Changing Lanes for Business

4 Simple Steps
to Overcome Problems, Accelerate
Progress, and Achieve Your Goals!

Tim Rhode

ISBN: 9798862705133 (Paperback)
ISBN: 9798866060184 (Hardcover)

For business leaders everywhere
who want a reliable way to get
from where they are—to where they want to be.

CONTENTS

FROM THE AUTHOR

We don't need more complexity. We need simplicity. "Changing Lanes" is a metaphor for the familiar approach you use when driving, to develop the clarity, confidence, and agility that are essential in today's challenging business world.

My goal with this book and coaching program is to provide you with 4 simple and memorable steps to lead successful change... To make progress *whenever* you want, for the rest of your life.

To your success!

Tim Rhode

THE PROBLEM

Stuck and Frustrated
with Lack of Progress

Chapter 1

FLATLINING

Charlie awoke uninspired. Not depressed, really, just "normal." No fire. No excitement. Fairly low-energy and low-motivation. Without consciously noticing the malaise or lack of enthusiasm, he began as usual, going through the motions, getting ready for yet another day in what had somehow become an increasingly nondescript and unremarkable life.

He grabbed a shower, got dressed, and finished his morning routine, which had become just a quick cup of coffee, kissing his wife goodbye, and wishing the family a good day. At least those who were up. Then out the door to slog his way through traffic with the rest of the morning commuters.

Today, he was running about 10 minutes behind schedule and traffic was heavy. On days when he got off to a late start, mounting traffic would compound his delays and set him back before he even got started at work. It looked like another one of those days.

But Charlie had become artful at navigating his way. From experience, he had noticed patterns in traffic, and by looking ahead, had developed a sense of when and where things could slow down.

He saw it as a challenge. While he occasionally got stuck, his forward-focus often enabled him to change to a lane that was moving better than the rest.

As he drove, Charlie thought about his life. While it used to be filled with enthusiasm and achievement, it had gradually become an exercise in frustration. Interestingly, that frustration had come in the wake of his progress and promotion. As he'd risen through the ranks from a talented technician to a senior manager, his income grew, but so did his responsibilities. To the point that they seemed to outpace the pay, and rarely offered the sense of satisfaction that he had enjoyed in his earlier roles.

It wasn't that he lacked success. Because of his progress, rising through the ranks, he was generally viewed in the company as a successful leader. But lately, several projects had slowed or stalled. His department was getting mixed results and, overall, his numbers were flat, well below expected growth goals.

To make matters worse, it seemed he was facing increasing resistance, from both new and long-term members of his team, to changes he believed were necessary to keep pace and thrive in their rapidly changing market. In some cases, he wasn't quite sure what those changes should be.

Something was missing. Privately, he wondered if *he* was the issue. Had he risen to his level of incompetence?

His rare bursts of inspiration and joy these days were soon swamped by mounting responsibilities and what had unconsciously become an unproductive routine. Growing frustration came from week after week, and in some cases, year after year of "*not*"... things at work and home *not* being as good as they *could* be. Certainly *not* the way he really wanted them to be. And *not* making progress on the priorities he was most passionate about.

Preoccupied with thoughts about the day's dilemmas and his mundane existence, he failed to notice a long line of brake lights ahead, and soon found himself stuck in a lane of stopped traffic. Only the far-left lane seemed to be moving. He cursed his luck, longing to be where others were moving forward. But he was solidly trapped. Perhaps, in more ways than one.

After what seemed like an eternity, the traffic began to move, and Charlie, paying more attention now, was able to make up some lost time. When he finally arrived, he was only 10 minutes late, but the words of his very first boss rang in his ears... "*If you're not 10 minutes early, you're late!*" Charlie regretted not leaving sooner to allow for traffic tie-ups, but he had stayed up late watching TV the night before and needed every extra minute of sleep he could get. Perhaps he'd hit the snooze button once too often.

As he reached his desk, he rolled up his sleeves, thinking things would improve when he got to work on his plans for the day... right after he checked his email and other incoming communication.

Instead, they got worse. Much worse.

His first clue was that he had already received 29 new messages. Really? Did the world *need* to reach him 29 times just since yesterday evening? Why did it seem these days that email was such a drag? In the early days it was a quick and efficient means of reaching people; a great means to expedite communication and progress. But over time, it had become an even better way for the world to bog him down with unsolicited offers, more information than he could process, and problems that others wanted him to solve. Despite his frequent unsubscribing and setting rules for priority messages, his inbox had become an endless to-do list for other people's urgent priorities.

As he dealt with the junk, he came across four messages that hijacked his day – two of which he had to address right away. Two of his best people were at odds about how to approach an important project. Really, they were at odds with each other. He had inherited this team, and with it, an ongoing drama of disagreement and disregard between these two on anything the other said or did. He often had to invest significant time and energy getting them to play nicely.

Another message would hold up this week's progress. A key member of the team had become ill. She would miss at least four days in the office and could not work from home.

The final curveball, although it was still early, replaced his day's priorities with someone else's. It came from his boss, who had called an afternoon meeting of the senior team to address a new project that had suddenly become a priority. "So much for a plan," Charlie thought.

He responded to the ill team member, sent his well-wishes, and requested some information that would allow them to make progress in her absence. He wasn't expecting an immediate response, so he finished dispatching his email and set off to visit the two warring teammates about their issues. He'd learned long ago *never* to address disagreements via email.

After meeting with them individually, he brought them together, diffused the disagreement, and helped them with a plan they both agreed to follow. "At least for now, Charlie thought. "We'll see how long this lasts." Their thinly disguised contempt was palpable.

It was nearing time for lunch, and Charlie was already spent. Occasionally, when he took time to reflect, he could recall when it wasn't like this. He used to be energized by work. There had been many years when he had acted freely, pursuing and often exceeding his business and personal goals. While the new reality seemed to sap his energy, there was a part of him, he sensed, that was still alive. Still passionate. Still hopeful. Still believing things could be different. Better... That there *was*, in fact, a way for him to escape the stuck-ness that had come to define his existence.

He needed a break to clear his head. Fortunately, there was a coffee shop downstairs with grab-and-go food that he could eat quickly or bring back to his desk, where he would work through lunch to prepare for the unplanned meeting.

What he didn't know was that on this day, seemingly destined to become another unremarkable mile along his journey, he would discover a way to break free from mediocrity – a way so simple and easy that he couldn't believe he hadn't seen it or thought of it sooner.

Chapter 2

HELP ARRIVES

At the coffee shop, Charlie grabbed a juice drink and a sandwich that he hoped would curb his hunger. He needed to focus on preparing for the meeting with his boss and couldn't afford to have his stomach distracting his brain. While lost in thought about his hunger and the upcoming meeting, he gradually noticed a familiar face smiling at him from farther up the checkout line.

Bill had overseen Charlie's department and led the team that recommended him for his first management role. Bill had soon been promoted to vice president for business development, and then senior VP, reporting directly to the company president. Since Bill moved to a different location, Charlie hadn't seen him for nearly two years.

Once he'd checked out, he noticed Bill waiting for him. He went over to say "Hi," but Bill started the conversation first. "Charlie, it's great to see you! I've been keeping track of your progress, and it seems like you're doing great things."

Charlie certainly didn't feel like he was doing great things, especially today. Rather than complaining, he simply said "Thanks," and expressed his appreciation for Bill's initial recommendation.

Bill replied, "It was *your* talent and energy that got you that role. Not my recommendation. How's it going? I know that department can be challenging at times."

Knowing he had to get back to prepare for the meeting, Charlie was tempted to end the conversation there by just saying "Fine." Or even sugar-coat it and say something like "Things are going really well." But they really weren't.

For some reason, Charlie had always felt comfortable around Bill. Even though he was now part of senior management in the company, Bill had a way of making people feel comfortable. It was a gift that Charlie was sure had much to do with Bill's achieving a senior leadership role. Feeling safe with Bill, Charlie opened up, just a bit. "We made some early progress, but lately, our results have been mixed," he confessed.

As if he sensed that Charlie could use a hand, Bill paused, looking at the food they were both holding, then said, "I'm guessing we both came here for the same reason. Let's find a place to sit where we can enjoy this gourmet lunch and you can fill me in." Charlie grinned and nodded at an open booth.

Once they were settled, Bill began to reassure Charlie that all departments and management roles had challenges and tended to make uneven progress. "That's where promising leaders like you come in," said Bill.

Sensing the value in Bill's counsel, Charlie went a step further. Not being one to complain, he briefly described some of the frustration he was feeling. From time wasted on projects that didn't bear fruit to working with team members who were disengaged, under-performing, and slow or reluctant to embrace change. Even his commute this morning had been a challenge. And over time, these things had worn down his normal energy and resilience.

Many people take the wrong view of change.

Hearing Charlie's dilemma, Bill smiled again and mused, "Many people take the wrong view of change."

"Wow!" thought Charlie. That comment *certainly* took him by surprise. Even though *he* didn't resist change, he noticed reluctance from others, just about any time change was introduced.

Charlie replied, saying "Most people think change is hard."

"Only because they make it so," said Bill. "What is change but putting yourself, your team, or your company in a better position to succeed?"

Charlie hadn't really thought of it that way.

Bill said, "Change happens in people's lives every day. If you can't control the change, then you have to go with it and be in the best possible place with your attitude, intentions, and actions to make sure the outcome is positive. Any alternative to that is miserable."

That was profound, thought Charlie. But before he could comment, Bill went on:

"It's just like the traffic you ran into this morning. Tell me more about that?"

Charlie was taken aback that Bill had chosen to ask him about traffic rather than offer advice on handling the plots and drama developing at the office.

Instead of changing the subject, Charlie obliged and told Bill about leaving late, not looking ahead, getting stuck in stopped traffic, then slowly making his way to a lane that *was* moving in order to gain back some valuable time.

Bill replied, "You can navigate life and business much like traffic. Some things are within your control and others are not. You can't control how many people are on the road at 8 a.m., but you can control when you leave. You can't control that people are stopped in your lane, but you can change lanes to one that's doing better. Most of the time, the changes necessary to keep moving toward your goals in life or at work are well within your control and require no more effort than what you do to change lanes on the road."

"It's important to realize that helpful change rarely means a complete about-face," Bill said, "or even a major change of direction. In fact, most often, progress comes from sticking with your current direction, but changing lanes to be in the best position for success. Finding ways to do better, to go a little faster, to be more efficient, or more productive. Sometimes it means doing less of something or even slowing down. Once you see where you need to change lanes, navigating the path to your goals becomes much easier."

Charlie was stunned as the simplicity of Bill's advice began to sink in. While he didn't fully understand the analogy, there was something about it that just rang true. Charlie suspected that Bill's outlook on managing change easily had a lot to do with his success and cheerfulness. The guy seemed to handle *everything* with confidence and grace. Two traits he truly admired.

As they were finishing lunch, Charlie said, "This sounds so simple."

Bill replied, "It *is* simple. Over time, I've learned that there are just four important steps to changing lanes successfully. Once you get the hang of them, it's easy!" Bill concluded, glancing at his watch.

"I'd love to know more!" said Charlie, "but it looks like you might have to go."

"I do," said Bill. "There's a board meeting next week, and we'll be making some big decisions. I'm in town this week to prepare.

"In the meantime, we both have to eat, right? If you're available, let's meet here tomorrow at the same time and I'll start sharing those steps."

"I wouldn't miss it!" Charlie replied.

Bill stood, and as he reached for Charlie's hand to bid farewell, he said with a wink, "In the meantime, when you drive home tonight, pay attention to when and how you change lanes and how things turn out. Tomorrow we'll talk about how that can work for you here in the office and in other areas of your life."

As Charlie watched him walk away, he realized his energy was up. Just being with Bill and learning there was an easier way for him to succeed had fueled him with hope and anticipation. Just the kind of energy he needed to bring to the meeting at 1:30. Coming here for lunch today had turned out to be a great idea, Charlie mused as he cleared their table and made his way back to the office.

Charlie prepared as best he could for the afternoon meeting, reviewing his department's performance and challenges, along with the company's mission and goals for the year. They were important factors when considering new projects and directions.

It turned out that the meeting was about a new acquisition opportunity. One that would mean significantly more work for Charlie's team at a time when they were already underperforming. At least by his standards. Not wanting to hinder the enthusiasm for the deal, Charlie asked a few thoughtful questions about timing, resources, and expected outcomes that were well received and showed why he had been invited.

After some discussion, the decision was made to recommend the acquisition to the board. The meeting ended with great enthusiasm, but inwardly, Charlie felt even more uneasy. In the back of his mind, he knew there would need to be some significant changes in order for him and his team to rise to the new challenge and perform well.

The rest of his day was less eventful, but he spent his time wisely, checking in with each of his key people, starting with the two he'd met that morning about their disagreement. While he sensed there was still resistance, he was pleased to find they were making some progress. That was welcome news.

While he wasn't at liberty yet to let the team know about the possibility of an acquisition, his communication with the rest of the team was a bit of a roll call to develop an accurate sense of where they were solid and where he would need to provide support or change.

Charlie worked about a half-hour longer than usual, distilling a list of strengths, weaknesses, needs, and goals for the new scene that might unfold. He was glad to have that done but cursed silently when he looked at his watch and realized that once again, he would be in the thick of traffic heading home. On the way to his car, he reflected on his conversation with Bill and remembered his assignment: *"Pay attention to when and how you change lanes and how things turn out."* While he wasn't exactly sure what Bill wanted him to see, once he was on his way, he approached it like a driving instructor, breaking down the process so they could continue their conversation tomorrow. By the time he arrived home, he thought he had it figured out.

Charlie's family had a tradition. During dinner, each member of the family would describe how their day went, ending with a valuable lesson they'd learned. While sometimes their contributions were a stretch, Charlie and his wife were determined to raise their family with a positive outlook and a love for learning. This evening, when it was Charlie's turn, he mentioned the usual challenges and obstacles, but minimized them. Instead, focusing on how good it was to see Bill again and his eagerness to learn from a master about how to deal effectively with change. From there, the conversation fell into good humor with each member of the family sharing changes they looked forward to vs. the ones they normally dread.

The rest of the evening was uneventful. After cleaning up from dinner, the kids went off to their rooms for some time alone, to play games or do homework, while Charlie and his wife settled onto the couch for some "quality time". Which, these days meant watching TV together while scrolling on their phones. They went to bed at the usual time. As he went to sleep, Charlie couldn't stop thinking about his chance meeting with Bill and what he would learn tomorrow.

Chapter 3

READY TO LEARN

When Charlie awoke the next day, he didn't hit the snooze button, but found he was in much the same place as yesterday. Still flat and uninspired with the weight and uncertainty of the persistent challenges at work dominating his mind. Even more so now with a new acquisition pending. It seemed there were always more problems than solutions. He had to find a way to conjure up some energy.

The cynic in him thought: "S.O.S." Code for *same old sh*t*.

Except, not quite…

Today wasn't quite as bleak. Somewhere in the dreary fog of his deepening challenges, there was a ray of hope. He wondered whether the S.O.S. mentality was an honest assessment, or if it had become a bad habit he had unwittingly developed about his current plight.

"Plight," Charlie thought. That's an interesting perspective. Had he come to look at his career as a plight? Was it something being put upon him? No one made him take this job, or even work in this field. No. It was his choice… along with the way he chose to view it.

"You choose your attitude," Charlie thought, snapping out of his funk. Something in the back of his mind told him to table his thoughts and get on with the day.

He didn't want another late start, so he finished his coffee, said his goodbyes, and headed for the door. Luckily, he was still on time. Even a few minutes at this time of day could make a big difference in how well the traffic would be flowing.

During the drive, his mind cycled between how to handle his challenges and how he changed lanes in traffic. He focused enough on his driving that by the time he arrived at the office, he was sure he could respond well to Bill's questions about changing lanes.

Charlie settled into his office ready to start on his plan for the day. He *always* had a plan. As usual, he checked his email before starting, just in case there were any pressing items or, like yesterday, fires to put out.

Of course, there were. His home-bound team member replied she would not be able to provide the needed information he'd requested. Charlie understood but would now have to find a workaround. The project could *not* afford to stall.

In addition, there were several new threads of email about the pending acquisition. As a member of the senior team, he was compelled to read and, in some cases, weigh in with his own perspective.

By the time he finished, half of his morning was gone. He now had to try and cram his morning goals into the remaining few hours, or risk falling behind by afternoon. Charlie ramped-up his determination. He'd done it before and would do it again. He knew that dashing through his plan and priorities could compromise quality. So, he was careful to strike a balance between speed, efficiency, and effectiveness. It didn't pay to go fast if you turned out garbage.

He was so focused on his priorities that he lost track of time. Glancing at his watch, he realized it was nearly time for lunch. He put down his work, grabbed his notebook, and hustled down to the coffee shop to find Bill there, already in line.

Today they each chose a salad and water and headed off in search of a seat. They found a booth in the back and settled in to start their lunch and the next installment from Bill. It didn't take Charlie long to shift gears from his focus on work to the matter at hand. He was excited to continue the conversation with his old mentor.

First, Charlie asked how Bill was doing with his preparation for the board meeting. Bill revealed a little of what he was doing. Then, after some small talk, he returned to his assignment for Charlie from the day before.

"Okay," said Bill, "tell me about your driving experience since our conversation yesterday. Did you focus on what you do to change lanes?"

"I did!" said Charlie. He was eager to get into Bill's lesson.

"Great," said Bill. "What's the *first* thing you do? Give me the short version." Charlie was puzzled. The steps were so basic, there was *only* a short version. Even though they were simple, Charlie had written them down in his notebook and brought it with him, knowing there would be some insight and wisdom he wanted to record.

Steps to Change Lanes:
1. Make sure it's clear.
2. Signal
3. Look again.
4. Move into new lane.

He said, "First I check the next lane to make sure it's clear."

"Okay..." Bill said with some hesitation. "Then what?"

Charlie went on, "Next, I put on my signal."

"Good" said Bill, nodding for Charlie to continue.

"Then I check again to make sure it's still safe," he said. "Sometimes the opening goes away."

"Very good." said Bill. "Then what?"

"Then I move into the new lane."

"And that's it?" asked Bill.

"Yep," said Charlie, certain that he had covered it well.

Bill rewound the conversation. "Let's go back to the beginning." said Bill. "You left out an important step."

"What is it?" asked Charlie, somewhat surprised.

THE SOLUTION

4 Simple Steps to Lead Successful Change

Chapter 4

STEP #1:
DECIDE TO CHANGE

Bill said, "Today we should focus on the first step of a successful change."

Charlie could see this might take more than one conversation.

Bill went on, "I can see by the look on your face that you're wondering where this is going. Like I said, it's both simple and easy, but first you want to know and understand each of the steps and do them in the right order if you want things to work out well. Soon it will become so automatic that you won't even realize you're doing it."

Bill continued with a question: "When *do* you change lanes?"

Charlie thought for a minute then replied, "When I look ahead and, like you said, I see the need or an opportunity to keep from getting stuck or improve my progress. It's sort of automatic, I guess…"

"Really?" quizzed Bill. "You're right that there can be a need or an opportunity. But is it automatic? Do you *always* notice this in advance?"

"No," Charlie confessed. "Sometimes I *don't* see the need or opportunity till it's too late. Then I'm stuck, and I have to wait it out, or force a change."

"Sound familiar?" asked Bill.

Charlie huffed "It sure does. Like some of the challenges I'm facing right now."

"At least you're looking at them as challenges," said Bill. "That's a good sign."

"A good sign of *what*?" Charlie wondered.

"Recognizing a need or opportunity for change to overcome challenges is a vital role of leadership," Bill said.

He continued, "Without it, people, departments, and entire organizations become stagnant and live with dysfunction. It's important to keep an eye on the road ahead to look for needs and opportunities to improve progress. And sometimes to avoid catastrophes."

Charlie looked at Bill and replied, "That makes sense, but things are *constantly* changing. The economy is changing. Our market is changing. Our competition is changing. Our priorities, goals, budgets, and staff are changing. I feel like I'm trying to hit a dozen moving targets."

Then he added, with frustration, "With challenges from all that change, we struggle to make progress and achieve our goals. To even remain competitive, let alone striving to get ahead of the market and competition.

"Some of my biggest problems are the time wasters. Disruptions like unscheduled meetings, unplanned direction changes from senior leadership, key people out sick. An overloaded inbox, or energy vampires like feuding team members or people resisting change.

Sometimes I'm just not sure where to start, or how to fix things."

Charlie felt like he was having a pity party, so he stopped. Then said, "It's all resulting in a lack of fire, energy, enthusiasm, hope, and self-esteem. For me *and* the team. Does it really have to be this way? It shouldn't be so hard."

Bill looked at him with a sense of reassurance and said, "Charlie, nearly every business leader out there is facing similar challenges. And many are struggling. But making progress and achieving your goals *doesn't* have to be so hard.

"ALL Progress Requires Change"

"All progress requires change. It's the one thing necessary to fix or avoid your challenges, now, or in the future. In fact, leading successful change is *the* most valuable skill for business leaders in the market today. The good news is that you're already on your way to learning a simple approach to *succeed* with change.

"Even *better* news is that it's something that you already know how to do!"

He paused, then continued. "Let's get back to the most important part of Step #1 so you can get started with your decision - and then learn the other three steps."

Charlie took a breath and said, "Okay. What's the most important part of Step #1?"

Bill began, "It starts with what I asked earlier, about 'When *do* you change lanes?' You said, 'It's when you see the need or an opportunity to improve progress.' That's *part* of it... But you have to *decide* to change.

Spotting a problem or opportunity does nothing to improve your progress unless you decide to act on it. Looking ahead in traffic last night only made you more aware. It was only after you *decided to change* that you took steps to act on your decision, avoiding problems and improving your progress.

Not deciding to change is one of three main reasons why businesses, and business leaders, struggle and fail to achieve their full potential."

"Why would leaders not decide to change when they're struggling to make progress?" Charlie asked. Knowing before he even finished the question that he was describing himself.

"That's a great question." Bill replied. Most people *want* to do well. But being uncertain about what to do, or what they *can* do... Maybe lacking resources, options, support, or confidence, many leaders, whether consciously or unconsciously, just choose to remain stuck.

They'll say things like: "*That's just the way things are around here.*" Or blame their poor performance on circumstances or factors, conveniently beyond their control."

"You just described me!" Charlie admitted, thinking out loud about the lingering issues he'd been tolerating. So, how can I get past my uncertainty and make the changes we need?"

Bill replied, "It starts with a few simple questions *every* business leader should ask when they see the need or an opportunity for positive change."

Charlie grabbed his notebook and pen and said to Bill: "I'm ready!"

Bill began, "Question #1 is, 'Where are you now?'"

Charlie wrote it down, looking puzzled.

Bill said "Remember, we're replacing uncertainty with clarity. There isn't a navigation app in the world that can show you the way to your destination without knowing your starting point. Start by identifying the top struggles and pains that you believe need to be addressed to make progress, and why you're having them. You want to get *clear* about your current situation. You'd be surprised how many times business leaders focus more on solving symptoms than identifying the real cause."

"Don't get lost in the weeds on this." Bill added. Just a quick and honest assessment of your current situation will help you *and* your team decide to change.

"Okay" said Charlie.

"Question #2," said Bill, "is, 'Where do you want to be… What are your goals?' You can start with this if it's the first thing on your mind, then answer the first question."

He paused and added, "As long you get clear about the challenge and your ideal outcome. You're at A. Where's B? What do you want to achieve? And why?

"What do you want to achieve? And Why?"

"This is important!" Bill paused for emphasis. "Knowing *what* you want is not enough to ensure success. Understanding the *why* behind your goals provides the meaning that will help you to persevere and help others get on board, to propel you all in the new direction. Especially when you're feeling challenged."

Charlie nodded and said, "That makes a lot of sense!"

Bill continued. "The next question to ask is, 'What are your roadblocks?' What's hindering or delaying your progress? Is it people? Processes? Culture? Inconsistency? Resources? Maybe a lack of vision and attention? Or maybe all the above?! Listing the gaps and obstacles you see will help you understand challenges you're facing. Then decide whether to go over, under, around or through them as you "change lanes."

Charlie was writing as fast as he could when Bill said, "I have these questions on a simple worksheet I use whenever I sense the need or opportunity for change. If you'd like, I'll send it to you when I get back to the office."

"That would be great!" said Charlie. He felt like he was getting a real education. Like an eager student, Charlie said, "I know they'll be on the worksheet, but I'm curious… What are the other questions?"

Bill smiled and looked at his watch. "Sure," he said. "I have a few minutes yet. Let me give them to you quickly. Then you can use the worksheet to help you decide to change whatever would help you most!"

Charlie put down his pen and sat back to absorb, as Bill continued.

"Question #4 is about a solution: 'How to best get there?' What is your first idea for how to solve the issue? You don't need to work it all out at this point. Just capture your initial thoughts on how you can best achieve your goal(s) and avoid or overcome the consequences. A few minutes of brainstorming will give you a place to start. Plus, you'll have something to bounce off others who will either endorse and build on your approach or offer alternatives.

"And speaking of alternatives, Question #5 takes it a bit further: 'What are at least two alternative solutions?' This helps you keep an open mind and prevents you from getting trapped into believing that there is only one solution."

Bill continued, "Long ago, I learned from one of *my* old mentors that there are at least three solutions to any problem. I've made it one of my core beliefs. It has served me well over the years and led to many successes. In fact, any time I skip this step, I typically live to regret it."

"There are at least 3 solutions to any problem."

Charlie was blown away. What Bill had just shared off the top of his head really opened his eyes. It felt like he had just learned something he could use for the rest of his career to make better decisions.

Bill added: "Taking a few minutes to consider and answer these questions will give you the clarity you need to make a good decision and, in the next step, make a commitment about which direction, how much, and *when* to change. That's something most business leaders don't bother to do. Without a simple and reliable approach to lead successful change, they rely instead on their instincts or intuition and don't realize how limited they are by their own experience, exuberance, or apprehension."

Bill started to pick up his things and said to Charlie. "I've got to run, but I'm enjoying our conversation. Want to meet back here, same time tomorrow?" I'll give you the second step for leading successful change."

"I wouldn't miss it!" said Charlie as he thanked Bill. He finished clearing the table, then headed back to his office.

He was catching up on email traffic he'd put off from the morning when he saw a message come in from Bill with an attachment and cover note. It said:

> "*Hi Charlie,*
> *Really enjoyed our lunch! Here are the questions for* **Step#1 of Changing Lanes**. *Use them whenever you have something to fix, a challenge to overcome, or an opportunity to make progress. Your answers will not only help you to DECIDE whether to change but will also help you with the simple steps to follow...*
> Cheers!
>
> *Bill*"

"Simple enough," Charlie thought. He finished responding to only the most urgent and important emails, then closed that screen, silenced his phone, and turned his attention to the questions Bill had recited earlier and just sent with his email. Charlie could see it was really a worksheet that he could re-use, so he saved a master copy, printed one out, then went to work considering where to start. He had at least four big challenges, causing him to struggle, and pondered which to tackle first:

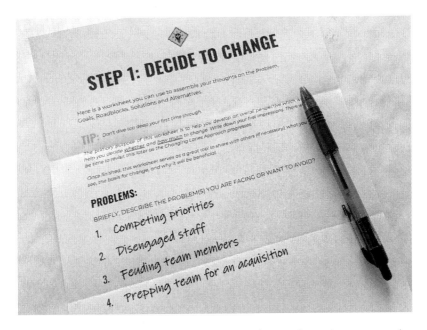

STEP 1: DECIDE TO CHANGE

Here is a worksheet you can use to assemble your thoughts on the Problem, Goals, Roadblocks, Solutions and Alternatives.

TIP: Don't dive too deep your first time through.

The primary purpose of this worksheet is to help you develop an overall perspective which will help you decide whether and how much to change. Write down your first impressions. There will be time to revisit this later as the Changing Lanes Approach progresses.

Once finished, this worksheet serves as a great tool to share with others (if necessary): what you see, the basis for change, and why it will be beneficial.

PROBLEMS:
BRIEFLY, DESCRIBE THE PROBLEM(S) YOU ARE FACING OR WANT TO AVOID?

1. Competing priorities
2. Disengaged staff
3. Feuding team members
4. Prepping team for an acquisition

Thinking it might be a key to resolving the other issues, he decided to start with disengaged staff, and began to jot his answers for the rest of the questions.

Until now, he had believed that engagement, or disengagement, was something each person mainly chose for themselves. But as he answered the questions, he realized there was plenty he had done in the past, and could do even more now, to influence and improve his team's engagement.

He got through the worksheet in less than an hour and was sure, more than ever, that he had made the right choice on where to start. While the problem was far from solved, the clarity he felt left him determined and motivated to make things better.

The energy he got from completing the quick exercise and his lunch with Bill propelled him through the afternoon. He not only finished everything he had planned for the day but had time before he left to gather his thoughts and priorities for tomorrow and the rest of the week.

That hadn't happened much lately. While it used to be part of his routine, as his role and responsibilities grew, it seemed he was spending more time reacting, just trying to keep up. It felt good to be ahead of the curve again, even if only briefly.

He wrapped up his work, including a call to the team member who was home on sick leave. He was glad to hear she would be back by the end of the week and told her he had some exciting things to discuss when she returned.

As he headed for home, Charlie was alert for traffic slowdowns. He had already made a few lane changes to improve his progress, when he realized what he'd missed earlier. It was suddenly so apparent.

Still thinking about the questions he'd answered and his conversation with Bill, he now understood that the first step to improving progress *was* actually deciding to change.

He also realized that when he failed to make that decision, or made it poorly, he would find himself stuck with the frustration and consequence of falling behind or being late.

He remained focused, deciding when to change lanes, and navigated the entire way without once getting stuck.

While he would normally come home preoccupied with open cycles at work and stressed from dealing with traffic, tonight he was smiling and moving with a spring in his step. His wife, Jill, noticed the difference right away.

"Good day?" she asked.

Charlie smiled and said "Well, it didn't start out that way. In fact, my morning was nearly hijacked again. But then I had my second lunch with Bill about managing change and things just seemed to go better after that."

"So... You have it all worked out?" she asked.

"Not yet," said Charlie. He's sharing it with me in installments. Today we talked about the first step of changing lanes. I used it all the way home and didn't get stuck in traffic one time."

"Wait," his wife said, "Bill is giving you driving lessons?"

"No," Charlie grinned again. "Bill says that managing change is one of the biggest responsibilities that leaders have. He believes that it doesn't have to be hard. And when you look at it like changing lanes in a car, it becomes simple and easy to do. So, the steps we use to change lanes while driving are the same ones we can use to succeed with change in business."

Jill was an accomplished executive leadership coach and author and had recently launched her own successful publishing company. She'd used analogies many times herself to help struggling leaders understand new perspectives, and quickly recognized the potential of Bill's simple approach to leading successful change.

Together they prepared dinner and once again had their family discussion. Charlie shared what he had learned so far about the first step for leading successful change, along with several questions from the worksheet. They all laughed, joking that from now on, they'd never be stuck in traffic again!

As he went to sleep that night, he thought about his decision to improve the engagement of his team. While he didn't know exactly what it would take, he knew it was essential for their progress and future success.

Charlie awoke the next day, a few minutes ahead of his alarm, feeling good. As he showered and dressed, his usual sluggishness was gone. He noticed that just finishing his work and having his next meeting with Bill to look forward to, lifted his spirits.

It seemed like his sense of purpose had returned now that he had decided to lead this change. The potential of what Bill was teaching him gave him hope that he would soon have a way to overcome the challenges he was facing and get back to making remarkable and reliable progress.

On his way in, he continued to look ahead for traffic and opportunities to change lanes and maintain or improve his progress. What he'd already learned was helping, with both his progress *and* his attitude.

Thinking about how he could boost engagement with his team, he lost focus on the flow of traffic and missed a lane change or two that delayed his progress. So he looked for the next opportunity to get into a better lane, and was soon back on track for an early arrival.

Rather than becoming irritated, he smirked, realizing that the delays had really been a good omen... Little reminders to stay focused and change lanes thoughtfully, to maintain or regain progress and avoid frustrating slowdowns.

Then, he had a revelation. If looking ahead for opportunities to do better had improved *his* progress and spirit, what would it do for his team? His certainly wasn't the only perspective that mattered. He decided on the spot, to see what would happen if he asked every member of his team for their view as well.

Now he was *excited* to get to work. Not only to see what his team came up with, but also to learn from Bill what else he may be missing.

When he arrived at the office, he went through his usual routine, which included checking for new email and other messages. Sure enough, there were plenty. There were even a few that stood out as important. But so was spending time with his people. He liked to invest time with each of them frequently. Today he had even more of a reason to do so.

He decided the email fires could wait and set about tracking down each member of his team to check on their progress and challenges. And also, to find out what changes *they* thought would help their projects, department, or the entire company to improve.

That was a pretty profound question, so he was careful to be fairly casual with it. He didn't want to cause a stir or give people whiplash with a sudden change of direction. He just wondered what *they* might see that he could be missing.

The conversations went well but had mixed results. Some responses, typically from his top performers, were effusive. Most had several ideas on how to improve.

Others were less forthcoming. Either they had some reluctance to share their views, or they had simply never considered the question, leaving "the vision thing" to the boss. So, he assured them that it was not only safe to share their observations, but that he *wanted* their perspective.

He also paid attention to their apparent engagement with the current project, with him, and with their role overall. Comparing what he saw with what he thought they were capable of and with what was *really* needed.

While he had to be patient with some, in the end, every single person had shared at least one thing that could lead to improvement.

He thanked everyone for their input and promised to keep them informed and involved if any action was to be taken on their ideas. "What a gold mine," Charlie reflected. "And it's been here all along!"

"Many hands make light work, and many perspectives provide a more complete picture," Charlie thought. He wasn't sure how best to do it, but decided, right then, that he would find a way to continue to capture his team's views on possible improvements in their operation. Building trust that their ideas for positive change would always be welcome.

By the end of his visits, Charlie realized that, compared with their potential, his team's performance wasn't anywhere near a 10. More like a 6 or 7. And there was plenty of room for improvement. It was better for some and worse for others, but he knew they all wanted to perform well and help the team to win.

The conversations had also helped to improve his awareness of where they were in good shape for the acquisition and where they might need to make some changes.

He was looking forward to sharing his decision and observations with Bill at lunch when his phone buzzed. It was Bill texting him that he had a meeting at 1:00 and asking if Charlie could meet him now for an early lunch. Eager to keep the process going, Charlie replied "Yes!" then grabbed his worksheet from the day before and headed to the coffee shop.

When Bill arrived, he thanked Charlie for his flexibility, explaining that the president had called an impromptu meeting about the pending acquisition.

Charlie told him not to worry, explaining how grateful he was that Bill was dedicating so much time to helping him with this new approach.

They both accepted each other's appreciation, then grabbed a light lunch and headed to their favorite table. Being earlier than normal, they largely had the room to themselves.

Before Bill could ask, Charlie said, "Thanks for sending the questions from yesterday. I used it like a worksheet and spent the afternoon filling it out."

Bill replied, "It *is* a worksheet, of sorts. I made it for myself to use whenever I have a frustrating problem or opportunity that requires change."

"Did it really take you all afternoon?" Bill asked with his eyebrow raised.

"No!" laughed Charlie. "I was actually through it in less than an hour. But boy, did it open my eyes!"

Bill smiled and asked, "How so?"

Charlie replied "It had me thinking about things I wouldn't normally have considered. First, I had to decide which of our problems and challenges to even start with. While I need to see them all improve, it was a great exercise in setting priorities."

Bill picked up Charlie's worksheet, reading his notes at the top and his answer to the first few questions.

"Looks like you've decided to improve your team's engagement," Bill observed. "That's a great place to start. Especially when

40

you have a list of other things to improve or changes that need to be made. Business is a team sport. It's easier to win, and much more fun, when your team is all-in!"

Then Bill asked, "I'm curious. How did you find the questions?"

Charlie replied, "Some were easy. Some really made me think. And some were a real gut-punch. Like the 'Why' question behind our problems. Especially when I got honest about it. The one about roadblocks and obstacles helped me to see where our challenges *really* are. I even came-up with some alternatives in case my first approach doesn't go as planned."

"So, what were your main take-aways?" Bill asked.

"Three," Charlie said, holding-up three fingers, curling them down one-at-a-time as he listed them: "Clarity, Priority, and Commitment."

He continued, "There's no question that I now have a *much* better grasp of the issues. And, that this is my top priority. Answering these questions, and given the stakes and benefits, I'm *committed* to making this happen!"

Bill nodded with a smile and said, "Sounds like you've hit the spot."

Charlie could see the pride and approval in his expression.

Then Bill continued, "Speaking of hitting the spot, I'm hungry. Let's eat, and I'll share Step #2 of changing lanes. I have to get to the meeting a few minutes early. Liz wants me to weigh in on a few points."

Liz had been the president for nearly 10 years, and the company had done exceedingly well under her leadership. Maybe "under" wasn't the right word. Liz led from the front, but you never felt subordinate in her presence. She believed that the team, especially the front line, was the key to the company's success. And she always seemed to be a step or two ahead with what the business needed.

It was a great place to work.

Heck, it was a great place to thrive, Charlie corrected himself.

Chapter 5

STEP #2:
LOOK FOR OPTIONS
AND RISKS

They ate in silence for a few minutes, then Charlie asked, "What now? What's the next step?"

Bill finished his drink and replied, "That's easy!"

Then he continued with a question of his own. "When you're driving, and decide to change lanes, what's the very next thing you do?"

Charlie had been waiting for this and knew he had the answer. "I look to see if it's clear!" he declared.

"That's right!" Bill agreed. "And *where* do you look?"

Charlie thought the question odd and cocked his head as he replied, "Well, in the direction I plan to head," he said with some hesitation, concerned that there was something else he had overlooked.

Sensing his trepidation, Bill continued, "In addition to the direction you have planned, are there other places it's important to look, to determine your options, timing, and to avoid putting yourself or others at risk?"

Charlie couldn't argue with that and just nodded in agreement.

"It's not complicated," Bill continued, "but it *is* important for a business leader to look at more options than the first one that comes to mind."

As he finished, Bill reached into his pocket, pulled out a folded page, and slid it over.

Charlie opened it and read the top. It said, "**Step #2 Look for Options and Risks.**"

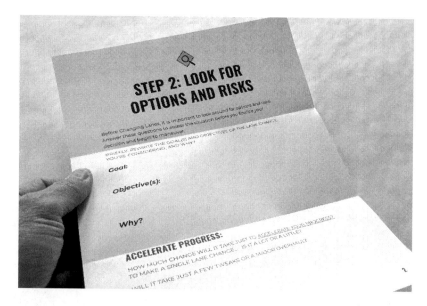

"Pretty appropriate title," Charlie commented.

"It is!" Bill replied. "Just a few more simple questions to make sure we know the options and risks *before* we change lanes."

Bill began to wrap up the rest of his lunch and said, "Now that you've decided to improve your team's engagement, take a crack at those questions and meet me back here tomorrow at our usual time. I'll be interested to see what you find."

Then he added, "They may not all apply to the change you've committed to making. But like checking a blind spot, you should at least look to see if they're relevant."

Bill glanced at his watch. He was right on time. Charlie thanked him again for being so generous with his time and wisdom. Bill just smiled and said, "You're worth it." Then turned and walked away.

Charlie reflected for a moment on how fortunate he was to have a mentor like Bill. He hadn't even asked for help, yet here he was... A senior VP, whose time was worth a fortune, sharing priceless lessons and assuring Charlie that "he was worthwhile."

Not only was he grateful, but he also felt affirmed and appreciated. Bill believed in him, and Charlie was determined to do his best and prove him right. As he turned to head back to his office, he suddenly realized that his *own* engagement was improving.

Just days before, he was flat and frustrated with his results, his team, and maybe even his job. After a few conversations with Bill, he was "all-in" and focused on making improvement. This wasn't just a clue. It was a neon sign, flashing right in front of him.

He imagined as he hurried back to his office that the sign might read: "CHANGE LANES NOW!"

He was eager to go through the questions Bill had shared, but with his early lunch, Charlie had a stack of work to catch up with.

With his focus and determination on high, he powered through it all, answering or deleting the rest of the messages he'd received. Then looked at his watch. He still had some time in his day and wondered if he could get through Bill's questions in an hour or less. So, he jumped in and finished 20 minutes before he'd planned to leave for the day.

He sat back and took the time he had left to reflect on his answers to the simple questions for Step #2.

The worksheet began by having him restate his goal and objectives, which helped him to confirm and get clear about what he *really* wanted to accomplish. He also tightened it up, adding some specific objectives.

His goal was "To improve the engagement of my team."

The two specific objectives he listed were:

1. "Improve morale and energy, camaraderie, and cooperation (*especially between my two feuding team members*)."

2. "Get back to the measurable progress and remarkable results we can produce for the company.

For "Why?" he wrote: "An engaged team is far more likely to succeed and contribute to solutions than one that is not. It's also more energizing and fun than being part of one that's disengaged and focused on struggles and problems."

"Like they are now," Charlie thought.

The first two questions on the worksheet helped him to get even *more* specific.

Number 1 was "How much change will it take to just improve progress?"

Not much, Charlie thought. If he could:

a. Get his two feuding team members to collaborate. Then

b. Have the team focus and hit at least one goal in the next 2-4 weeks,

   ...that morale would quickly improve.

They would not only remove a roadblock, but also help to develop some confidence and momentum heading into a potential acquisition.

Number 2 was "How much change to actually *achieve* the goal?"

At first, Charlie wondered how he would know when his goal was achieved. Then it dawned on him that the answer was simply the *opposite* of what he had now.

- The team's energy, collaboration, and morale would be consistently high.

- They would exhibit a can-do / will-do mindset, with no apparent reluctance, when it came to handling change and all that would come with the acquisition.

- And finally, they would reliably achieve their goals, on time or ahead of time.

While that seemed like a long way from where they were now, Charlie was determined to make it happen.

The next section addressed the "**Risks of Change.**"

The first question, "Will the change you intend add or diminish risk (short or long-term)?" was easy, Charlie thought. While he knew that some changes, like an acquisition, brought plenty of risks, there was *no* risk in improving his team's engagement, short or long-term. It was all upside, unless he had someone who wouldn't step up. Then *other* changes would need to be made.

While answering the next one, "Will it save time or take your time?" he had a revelation. Charlie initially thought he would have to put extra effort into his leadership. But then realized that if he just did a few things differently, like getting the team's input on how to do better and what they could all do to handle the acquisition and still achieve their goals, things would improve. It might require him to be more thoughtful, but *not* to necessarily do more work. So, he wrote "*No significant change in time required.*"

On "Will it make things easier, or harder at first before they get easier?" Charlie wasn't sure. He wrote: "*Perhaps a bit harder since I have to be more thoughtful about my leadership approach and communication. But if (or when) it starts to work, things will get much easier.*" He emphasized and underlined the word "*much.*"

Regarding "What resources or support he would need to succeed?" he thought, at first, that he would just rely on the way he led the team. On the inspiration and energy he could foster. But when he read the question again, he realized that there *were* resources and support that would be both necessary *and* helpful.

He listed them:

1. Talk privately with key opinion leaders on the team who would be willing to support and help lead the change once they know the plans and the "why" behind them.

2. Get the team out of the office for an informal happy hour to acknowledge their current challenges and express my appreciation for their dedication. Plus, my faith that as a team, we can turn things around. This will mark the beginning of our rally.

3. Invite senior leadership members to drop in on team meetings occasionally to share insight and express their appreciation and importance of our team's work.

4. Invite Bill, and even Liz, to visit the team when the time is right, to share the details of the acquisition and offer an executive briefing to emphasize the importance of the role we would play in making the acquisition a success.

As he wrapped up his initial list, he suddenly realized that those resources had been there all along! Why hadn't he seen them? Answering this question had pushed him to look beyond his current focus, which had narrowed as the team's progress began to drag. With his creativity set free, he suddenly felt like he had access to all kinds of resources and assistance that had become a blind spot for him.

Speaking of blind spots, the next two questions he didn't expect at all. Especially the first:

"How will it affect your personal life?" As he connected the dots, he began to see a circle, or perhaps a cycle that had started: Being on track to miss a goal or target drove him to narrow his focus and work harder.

He also drove his team harder. If (or when) that didn't pay off, and the goal was missed, the team's energy and morale slipped. Their spirit declined, and the workload seemed even more challenging.

Then the cycle repeated.

When it happened again, things slipped even farther.

Eventually, *perhaps every step of the way*, Charlie admitted that in the process, his personal life had also taken a hit. Maybe a few hits. His energy had declined. He was having less fun. And he was probably less fun to be around. The enjoyment and energy he used to feel had all but left the building.... Until he'd run into Bill and started learning about changing lanes.

As the lightbulb went off, Charlie realized that he and his team had unwittingly drifted into a slow lane. He began to feel that if he could lead his team through a few simple steps to change lanes, their energy and enthusiasm would return, along with his!

He was eager to meet with Bill the next day and share his revelations.

The next question, "How will your change affect others?" was something he always considered when leading change, but not as thoroughly as the list the worksheet offered.

Nor had he ever taken the time to write his answers. It had always just been in his head. Or, partially in his head. Never as thoughtfully as this. It was a revealing exercise.

a. "Your business partners." Charlie wasn't a partner in the firm. Not yet anyway. So, he didn't have partners in the traditional sense. But he did have colleagues and co-workers who led other divisions at the same level as he did. He thought about it for a minute, then concluded that an improvement, and hopefully a surge, in his team's engagement, would only serve to help other divisions and the company overall. There was one colleague whom Charlie was very close with who had been dealing with similar issues. Charlie decided he would share what he had recently learned from Bill, and his plans, to see if he had any concerns or suggestions, and see if a similar approach might help his team as well.

b. "Your family." This one was easy... His wife had already noticed a difference in his energy coming home after just a session or two with Bill. He knew that success with this change would have a *big* effect on how he showed up at home, and how much more he would be available to focus on his family. That alone made the change worth doing.

c. "Your team." This one was even easier. They would be the biggest beneficiaries of succeeding with this lane change. He knew they were all capable and wanted to do well. He also knew that their success, or lack of it, either energized them or sapped their collective energy. If their slide continued, he had no doubt that some would start looking for work elsewhere. As if he needed it, this *increased* his determination and the commitment to his decision even further.

d. "Your vendors." There had been times when, due to his team's failings, they had to delay orders or beg to rush supplies that Charlie was sure had put a strain on some of his key vendors. He wanted the company, and especially his division, to regain 'preferred vendor' status with their consistency, volume, and innovation.

e. The final consideration for this section was both easy and hard: "Your customers and other stakeholders." The customer part was easy. Improving his team's engagement would speed up their production and improve customer service, helping them to both supply and support all customers: key accounts, regular customers, and new customers. The "other stakeholders" part made Charlie pause at first. As one or more came into view, his perspective as a leader broadened. While his team didn't come into direct contact with them, he realized that improving his team's engagement would improve relations with all. There was no downside.

1) Shareholders – If his team continued to struggle, shareholder value could suffer. When fully engaged, his team would be making contributions that increased shareholder value.

2) Lenders – The company didn't have a lot of debt, but he knew that lenders would play a major role in funding the acquisition. This was a time for his team to accelerate and surge ahead. Not to struggle.

3) It wasn't a stretch to see the Marketing and Sales Division as stakeholders. An improvement in his team's engagement and productivity would enable improved marketing and increased sales.

These questions had been a real eye-opener. Charlie developed a broader perspective on not only the impact of his leadership but also the difference a single lane change could make for so many people!

The next section, titled **"Resistance Busters,"** offered a checklist for "The Risks of NOT changing." Asking "What could happen if you hesitate, or fail to Change Lanes?"

Charlie immediately saw *why* they were "Resistance Busters." Checking even *one* of these would help to reduce or overcome any resistance to change.

And Charlie had checked them *all!*

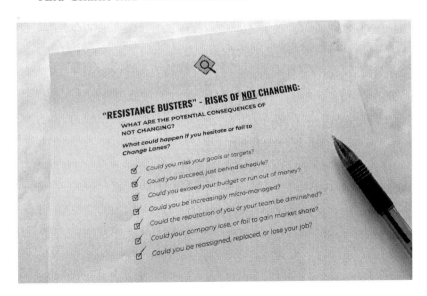

"RESISTANCE BUSTERS" - RISKS OF NOT CHANGING:
WHAT ARE THE POTENTIAL CONSEQUENCES OF NOT CHANGING?
What could happen if you hesitate or fail to Change Lanes?

- ☑ Could you miss your goals or targets?
- ☑ Could you succeed, just behind schedule?
- ☑ Could you exceed your budget or run out of money?
- ☑ Could you be increasingly micro-managed?
- ☑ Could the reputation of you or your team be diminished?
- ☑ Could your company lose, or fail to gain market share?
- ☑ Could you be reassigned, replaced, or lose your job?

The last two questions had him consider "Timing."

In the past, for any changes he'd made, or even considered making, he'd just used his instincts, based on urgency and his availability to focus on them. Looking at these questions in advance to determine the ideal timing seemed both deliberate and sensible.

His answer to the first: "Is it safe (or essential) to change lanes immediately?" was easy. A big "YES!" It was both safe *and* essential, in his mind… He wished he had changed lanes three months ago!

The second timing question was: "If not immediately, when would be the best time to start and finish the change?" Charlie could see that trying to make too many changes too soon, all at once, or even at the wrong time of year, could cause problems. He suddenly appreciated the importance of the question. There were other changes on his list from Step #1, like "preparing his team for the acquisition," that would benefit from considering this question.

That was a breeze, thought Charlie.

Some of the questions he would *never* have thought to ask. Although, he had to admit, they *did* make sense, especially the ones about how the change would affect others, and how it would affect his personal life.

He felt like his perspective had just been expanded and might never return to its original limits.

Before putting the worksheet away, he decided that he wanted to see if he could get his team's engagement back to where it had been, or even *better*, within three months. He went back to Step #1 and added that to his objectives.

That evening, he was fully present and engaged with his family, rather than having a portion of his attention still focused on struggles with the business.

The next morning, Charlie awoke filled with energy, ready and eager to get started. The questions Bill had offered for Steps 1 and 2 of changing lanes had given him the clarity and confidence to proceed.

On his way in, he realized that he had developed a much greater awareness of all that was going on around him when he decided to change lanes. Things happening in front, behind, and from the opposite direction were all important to consider if he wanted to change lanes successfully and not put himself or others at risk.

With that happening spontaneously, he realized what he *usually* did next, before actually making the change. He used his turn signal to alert other drivers of his intentions.

Charlie considered himself a safe driver. He had never caused an accident and hadn't had a ticket in more than 10 years.

But as he reflected on his steps to change lanes, he realized that his signaling was inconsistent. There were times he would signal well in advance, like he was taught in Driver's Education class, way back in the day. Other times, he would already be heading into the new lane before he started to signal. Not good.

And then there were times he changed lanes without signaling at all.

"Worse yet!" Charlie thought. Even when traffic was light, it meant he was being unpredictable to nearby drivers.

As he thought more about it, he realized there were two other signaling problems that often frustrated, or even angered him:

One was drivers who left their signal on, sometimes for miles, making everyone near them wonder if they were going to change lanes, or if they were just clueless.

The other example was when Charlie spotted an opening to change and signaled the drivers trailing alongside, who would then hurry to close the gap, blocking his path and holding up his opportunity to make progress. He'd seen people in business who resisted change do the same thing.

When he arrived at work, he wasn't sure where his lesson today would go with Bill. Still, he was eager to thank him for helping with the clarity and confidence in his decision to look at the options and risks and see whether signaling was part of the changing lanes process. It *had* to be, Charlie thought.

Energized by his decision to change lanes, Charlie hit the ground running. Then reality set in.

Making his rounds, he quickly realized that the feud between his two team members was back on. This time it not only affected the two people involved but put his whole team on edge. He did his best to head it off and get everyone back on track, but their simmering disagreement was a real energy drain, and had to stop.

Then the quarterly reports arrived. Charlie knew without looking that the news would not be good. They weren't the worst performers in the company, but they were far from the best. And they were producing well below their capability.

As if he needed any more incentive, here were two sobering reminders of the need to change lanes and improve progress. While events like these would have normally been demoralizing, this time they only served to increase Charlie's determination and commitment.

He drilled into the numbers, confirming where his team needed the most improvement. Everything aligned with the goal and objectives he had already outlined.

The next thing Charlie knew, it was time to meet with Bill. He grabbed his worksheets from both Steps 1 and 2 and headed for the coffee shop.

Not seeing Bill, he grabbed a salad and a drink and staked out a table where he could see the entrance. It was uncharacteristic of Bill to be late. But they didn't exactly have a set appointment. Plus, it gave him a chance to review the questions and his answers. There were a few he wanted to tighten up. Especially given his experiences from the morning.

Five minutes later Bill walked in and spotted Charlie. As he approached, he immediately apologized for being late. But Charlie let him know that he didn't mind and had used the time productively.

Bill quickly returned with his lunch and, apologizing again, explained his delay.

He had been on an important call. Without naming names, he said there was a single board member potentially holding up the acquisition. From Bill's perspective, it was largely because the board member felt he hadn't been advised or consulted properly about the basis, and benefits the company would gain from the acquisition. Bill contacted him to provide the missing information and didn't want to end the call without making *sure* he was both comfortable and on board with the offer. When Charlie asked if he had been successful, Bill nodded, then explained that after he had won his support, they spent extra time discussing how the board member could also help to ensure the success of the acquisition with all of his contacts and resources.

Before starting in on his lunch, Bill asked if Charlie had worked on the questions to **Step #2: Look for Options and Risks** that he had shared yesterday. Charlie smiled, sliding his completed worksheet across the table. Bill read it, nodding, as he ate.

When he finished reading, he looked up at Charlie and said, "You've done a really thorough job with this. Did the questions lead to any new insight?"

"Did they ever!" Charlie replied, sharing his revelations, realizing the resources and support he would need, or already had... Especially the Resistance Busters and how improving his team's engagement would affect his personal life, and how it would affect others.

Summing up, Charlie said, "I realized not only the opportunities to succeed, but the risks involved if I don't. *I am committed to making this happen over the next 90 days.*"

Now Bill was grinning. They talked more about insights the questions for Step #2 had revealed.

As he finished his lunch, Bill changed the subject and asked Charlie what he thought the next step was.

Charlie had an idea and said, "The next thing I do when changing lanes is to *signal.*"

Chapter 6

STEP #3:
SIGNAL THE CHANGE

Bill slapped the table and said "Exactly right! I told you this was simple!"

"The challenge" he continued, "is doing it well!"

Charlie confessed that while he considered himself a good driver, he realized his own signaling was inconsistent, wondering whether that might also be the case with his leadership.

"We *all* want to think we're good leaders and good communicators." said Bill. "But even the best of us have blind spots. Unless we're willing to look for them and improve, or get help, when necessary, things will be predictably mismanaged."

He continued, "At the heart of *every* problem is poor communication. It's a major cause of resistance, struggle, and failure when trying to lead change. The *good* news is that it isn't hard to communicate well. It only requires three things..."

Charlie sat up, paying close attention. He had a sense this was going to be good.

Bill proceeded:

"Number 1, you've got to care. Realize that changing lanes without signaling properly is risky and reckless. It breeds reluctance, resistance, and even resentment from people who feel left out or take offense when you don't inform or include them. It also causes confusion and wasted time because people make uninformed decisions about what they should be doing.

"Number 2, you've got to be thoughtful. Look around and put a little thought into who would want or need to know about the change you're planning. It's also not just *who* you choose to inform. It's *when* and *how*. And,

"Number 3, you've got to actually *do* it... Be consistent. Continue communicating until your change is completed. This can make or break the success of your change. Do it well and your change will be much easier. Do it poorly and your change will either struggle or fail."

"Have you ever watched truckers passing each other on the highway? Bill continued. Those guys are pros. It's what they do for a living. What's the last thing they do when they finish the pass?"

Charlie thought a minute. He'd seen this many times, but never made the connection to business leadership. "When it's clear, the truck being passed flashes its lights to the one going by."

"Right," said Bill, "to signal that it's safe to pull back in. Then what?"

Charlie thought he'd nailed the answer, but when he thought a little further, he smiled, realizing what he'd missed. "The truck that finished the pass and got the 'all-clear' signal winks its light off and on to say 'thank you' for the help."

Charlie was beginning to realize that signaling – *communicating* – is as important to progress and success as the decision to change in the first place. But he was starting to think it seemed like a lot.

Bill noticed his expression change and said, "Don't worry. It isn't hard. In fact, it's easy, and can even be fun! Especially when you recall the importance of your change and the progress it will bring."

"Here's a quick checklist I've developed over the years that I *still* use to make sure I get this right," Bill said as he slid another folded worksheet across the table to Charlie.

As Charlie was scanning Bill's checklist, he said, "Really? You have a checklist for communication?"

Bill smiled and replied, "Absolutely. Most business leaders rely solely on their instincts and good intentions to guide them. Which explains why about 70 percent of change efforts in business struggle or fail. As good as they are, and there are great business leaders out there at *all* levels, a simple system to get this right will beat instinct and good intentions, every time."

"Think of commercial pilots that fly planes full of people, safe-ly, every day," Bill pointed out. "What do they do before, during, and after every flight?"

"They use a checklist," Charlie said, "to make sure they haven't missed anything."

"Right," Bill agreed. "They also communicate. To the ground crew, the flight crew, the tower, and the passengers. Before, during, and after *every* leg of *every* flight."

Charlie was beginning to see examples of good and responsible communication all around him.

Then, Bill hit him with a real gem. "Remember, we only change lanes to do *better*... No one changes lanes to do worse!

"We only change lanes to do *better*... No one changes lanes to do worse!"

Your mindset will drive your results here. View it as an *opportunity* to bring people into your plan and help with its success. Or, at least not to obstruct or put-up resistance.

"Use that checklist to guide you. There may be items on there that don't apply to the change you're planning now. Just ignore them. But don't decide to ignore them too quickly. This is where caring and being thoughtful comes in. Sometimes, with a little thought, a need or opportunity to communicate comes to mind that you didn't see originally.

"Likewise, keep your mind open for any helpful communica-tions that might not be on the list. I've improved this checklist over the years, but I'm sure you can make it better. *Forethought is much better than regret.*"

That really rang true to Charlie.

They had finished lunch and it was time for them to wrap up. As he folded the list and put it in his pocket, Charlie thanked Bill and told him he'd get on it right away. He then asked if Bill was available for lunch again tomorrow.

"I know you have that board meeting coming up," Charlie added.

Bill said "I wouldn't miss it. I'm working on another project and am really looking forward to seeing if that checklist to signal the change has been helpful for you."

They agreed to meet at the same time, then cleared the table and headed back to their offices.

Charlie couldn't wait to work through the checklist Bill had given him. Today's conversation really emphasized the importance of being a great communicator. He was beginning to see proper signaling as both a fun challenge and a responsibility. One he wanted to get right!

Returning to his desk, Charlie followed up on the commitments and conversations he'd had with members of the team during his morning rounds. Some needed information. Some needed approval. And others just needed affirmation. He'd found that a quick note expressing his appreciation for their good work went a long way to boosting their self-confidence and commitment.

Charlie had always felt that he was working *for* his team, rather than the other way around. While he owned the responsibilities of being the leader, setting direction, priorities, goals, and expectations, he saw it as his job to make sure that everyone on his team had what they needed to succeed. Including his encouragement. It seemed to work *much* better than the command-and-control approach used by many of the "bosses" he'd had in his career. He wanted his team working for the mission and the customers more than working for him. It was a perfect mindset for him to have as he opened the checklist for Step #3 of changing lanes.

Charlie considered himself to be a good communicator. But as he scanned the worksheet at lunch, he realized he *did* have blind spots – important communication that he wouldn't have normally considered. He was eager to jump in.

Signal the Change Checklist was divided into three clear sections: Who? How? And When?

The first of the Who questions was:

"Whose permission will you need?" While there were clearly changes or projects that Charlie would need approval or permission to launch, improving his team's engagement, morale, and productivity wasn't one of them. He left this blank.

The next Who question was:

"Whose help will you need?" While at first, he thought the change was all about him and the way he handled and inspired the team, he remembered his earlier idea about getting company leaders to visit and share information and appreciation for his team's work. So, he listed specific people, including Bill and Liz, who he would inform of his goal, and invite them and others to his team meetings.

It would help if he could get his feuding team members to bury the hatchet and collaborate productively, if not enthusiastically. Not sure whether that fell into this question, he wrote it down anyway and decided to discuss it with Bill.

He also remembered the two opinion leaders on his team who could not only influence everyone's buy-in, but also serve as a steady example as the team went through challenges that were sure to come with the acquisition.

He let his mind wander on the question for a while, not wanting to overlook anyone whose help he should consider. That helped him get creative.

Then it struck him that inviting some appreciative customers could help. Having them share how much they valued and appreciated the work his team did would go a long way to affirming their best efforts and determination to deliver and exceed expectations. They might even offer suggestions on what his team could do better.

He wasn't sure who he could get, or how he'd go about it, but wrote down the names of four or five key customers he would contact to see if they would be willing to visit and help with his plan.

He decided to keep his mind open for other possibilities but realized that just pondering this question revealed what had been a big blind spot for him. These resources had *always* been there. He'd just never thought of using them.

The best part was that all of this cost *nothing* to implement. He just had to see it and do it.

The next question was the exact opposite:

1. "Who could block or hinder your success?"

   Funny, thought Charlie… It could be some of the same people. He listed his two feuding team members. Their ongoing squabble would continue to waste time, sap energy, and undermine or tarnish any progress in morale and productivity.

   The opinion leaders were also pivotal. If they weren't on board, the lane change would be much more difficult. Getting their buy-in was critical.

   The fourth question was:

2. "Who else should be informed (supervisors, colleagues, subordinates, vendors, customers, etc.)?" Supervisors he'd already addressed. Then he thought about his peers, leaders of other departments and divisions at his level. Especially those whom his team worked with frequently. Letting them know of his intentions could only help to generate support and create a culture of success.

   Charlie had already thought about the vendors. While they didn't all need to be informed, there were several he would contact to let them know of his plans and ask for their assistance, addressing his team about their value and importance. By informing key vendors that he was raising the bar for his team's performance and asking for their feedback to confirm progress.

   Of course, there was his team itself. He would want to share his intention and goal for them to become more collaborative and productive and have that be firm but inspiring.

He also realized there were some other actions he could take to reinforce the new mindset. That was less about "who" and more about "how." Which happened to be the next question.

The worksheet then asked, "What are the best methods for each essential signal with the people, groups, or companies listed in the 'who questions above?"

The worksheet offered four main approaches:

- One-on-one: In-person, by phone, or via video conference.
- Group: In-person, with a team meeting, dinner, or happy hour, etc.
- Via email.
- Via video message.

As he chose the best approach for signaling each person or group he'd initially listed, he realized the importance of this step. *How* he would communicate with key people would play a big role in helping his lane change to succeed.

While Charlie's team used email and video messaging often, he knew that the communication he needed to have, at least initially, would best be live, in person. So, he listed those he wanted to meet with, one-on-one or in pairs. And which communications would be best done in a group, with just his team, with company leaders, vendors, or customers. Email and video messaging could be used later for updates and reinforcement.

The sixth and last question on the Signal the Change checklist was also about timing:

"When should you start to signal?"

It helped Charlie to realize that there may be some communication that should happen sooner, and other communications that might be better left until later, if not "just in time." As he planned the timing for his communication, he reflected on his past experience, both driving and, on the job, when communication was sent or received too late or too soon, and how it often disrupted progress and success with the intended effort.

The whole exercise for Step #3 took less than a half-hour.

When he finished, Charlie sensed how great it felt to have thought and planned this far through the improvements he wanted, and, frankly, *needed* to get back on the path to progress… All the way to having a plan for who, how, and when he would communicate with key people in order for this transformation to succeed.

With the worksheet complete and well over an hour left in his day, Charlie thought, "No time like the present." He decided to drop in on members of his team and use what he'd learned about Step #3 to start signaling and planting seeds for building their engagement and determination to succeed with their goals.

On his way home that evening, while paying attention to traffic and changing lanes to maintain his progress, Charlie reflected on how different he felt. In less than a week, he had gone from feeling hopelessly behind, frustrated, and dispirited, to being clear, hopeful, focused, and most importantly, confident that he could, and would, succeed with this plan to energize his team and be a model for the company.

That night at dinner, when it was time to share the highlights of his day, Charlie explained Bill's checklist for Step #3 and how just a few minutes spent planning had opened his eyes to the importance of good communication. Not only boosting the potential for his success with this project, but also having a new way to be a more thoughtful and thorough leader going forward.

The next day Charlie was eager to share his plans with Bill, to see if he'd gotten it right – then get started signaling the people whose help he would need to succeed.

He was also curious to learn about the fourth step that Bill had mentioned in their first meeting.

The morning went quickly as Charlie handled his administrative tasks and then made the rounds to see each of his people. While nothing material had changed, Charlie could see his energy reflected back at him from each of the team members he met. He began to wonder how much of the team's dismay had been caused by his own frustrations. He made a mental note to remain aware of the effect his attitude had on others, and always strive to keep his energy and positivity levels up.

While the acquisition had yet to be confirmed, he wanted his team to be ready to receive the news positively and step up to the demands that would certainly come.

When Charlie arrived at the coffee shop, Bill was already there, but on a call with his phone pressed to his ear. Charlie got his lunch and headed cautiously toward their table. He didn't want to interrupt. Bill looked up as he ended the call, smiling as he waved Charlie over and put down his phone.

Charlie started by saying, "I hope I didn't interrupt."

Bill said, "Not at all. In fact, that was the board member I spoke with the other day."

"The one who was not in favor of the acquisition?" Charlie asked.

"The same one!" Bill replied. "He was thanking me for the call. Since our conversation, he's realized the value of the acquisition and has offered his full support."

He looked Charlie straight in the eye and said, "That's the power of good communication."

Charlie nodded, letting Bill's advice sink in. He could tell that this would be a lasting lesson.

Before they even started eating, Charlie said, "That Signal the Change Checklist was a real eye opener for me!"

"How so?" Bill asked with a slight smile.

"I like to think that I'm a good communicator," said Charlie, "but the questions and suggestions on the checklist helped me to think, not just of other people I could or should signal about the change I want to make, but how and when as well."

"I hope it didn't take too long." Bill said.

"Not at all!" Charlie exclaimed. He added, "I was through it in 30 minutes. But holy cow! When I finished, I realized what I've been missing in the past, and what a difference this step will make.

Not just with *this* change, but *any* change I need to lead in the future."

Charlie slid his Signal the Change Checklist across the table for Bill to see.

"That's the beauty of the changing lanes approach," Bill said as he picked up Charlie's worksheet. "It will help with your success *every* time!"

As Bill reviewed Charlie's answers to the questions on the checklist, he nodded several times, then smiled as he saw his and Liz's names as the first two listed under who could help the change to succeed.

When he finished with the page, he put it down, looked at Charlie, and said "Two things...

"First, I *really* like the focus of your change. Improving the culture and mindset of your team is so important. It's what makes everything else possible.

"Second, the answer is 'Yes!' I would be delighted to communicate with your team members about the acquisition and their importance in our future success."

Charlie felt like he'd just hit a walk-off home run. He not only had Bill's affirmation about his decision to change lanes, but also his offer to help him succeed!

Charlie thanked him for his support.

They talked a bit more about Charlie's plans with his key people and feuding team members.

Bill even agreed to help secure Liz's commitment to meet with his team. "She loves communicating directly and sharing the company priorities." Bill said. "But she also doesn't want her trusted leaders to feel like she's bypassing them to speak with their teams. With your invitation and my encouragement," Bill said, "she'll be there with bells on."

Now Charlie was really stoked. He couldn't wait to get started!

Chapter 7

STEP #4:
CHANGE LANES

C harlie thanked Bill again, then said "So, what's the last step? I've been paying attention to my driving, and all that's left is to make the change."

"You're exactly right said Bill, smiling again. "But there's a bit more to it than that. In fact, the last step is where many business leaders and change efforts tend to struggle or fail."

Charlie was puzzled and asked, "How?"

"Before you launch, think of making the change as three parts," said Bill. "First is to plan the start. Determine the ideal pace and scope to begin."

"Then," he continued, "Ask yourself a few questions: "What is the right pace for the change you want to make? Is it incremental and gradual? Sudden and severe? Or somewhere in between?

"Should you accelerate to seize an opportunity or outrun the competition? Or slow down to get things right and improve efficiency and systems to ensure your eventual success?

"In traffic, we change lanes at a pace that varies depending on the situation. From gradually, when things are moving along and good options are obvious, to suddenly, when obstacles appear and opportunities to avoid them are urgent or fleeting. Then we have to change lanes quickly to avoid being stopped, delayed, or getting in a wreck.

"It's the same in business. But you want to know before you go," Bill continued. "Your answers will be determined by the size and scale of change you intend, and the urgency of the opportunities or obstacles you're dealing with."

Bill outlined a few questions about changes business leaders often face:

- Is there a timely opportunity to be the first mover into a new market space? Or would it be better to watch? To learn from others' efforts, then move in with a superior offering and dominate?

- Are the resources you'll need available to properly execute the change? Or will you be on a shoestring? (*Think people, financing, supplies, information, technology, marketing assets, etc.*)

- Is your team ready to move, or will you need to inspire, train, make additions, or changes before you head in the new direction?
- Is it possible for the change to be implemented over time to avoid disrupting harmony in operations? Or are you facing a sudden obstacle or issue that threatens your business, industry, or career?

"So, that's the pace," said Charlie. "What about the scope?"

"Well," Bill responded, "the scope is how much change? How far? And how severe?"

Bill continued, "Is it subtle? Do you just need to change one lane and stay there to improve progress and achieve the goals you have in mind? Or will you have to change several lanes to get things to the level you desire? Is it best to make those lane changes gradually, over time? Or all at once, to avoid catastrophe or further delay? Have you ever changed one lane, only to wish you'd have changed two? What's prudent, given the resources you have and consequences to the organization if you go too fast or slow? Too far, or not far enough?"

Charlie could see the sensibility of Bill's advice. He realized that in traffic, he made the same types of decisions in a split second, often unconsciously, to match the situation he was in.

This shouldn't be hard, thought Charlie. He did it many times every day when driving.

As he reflected on his lane change to improve the engagement and culture of his team, he realized that while it was both important and urgent, the best pace would be gracefully quick. Subtle but effective. He wanted to improve things ASAP, but not give the team whiplash with a sudden shift.

He also realized that changing one lane, to improve the culture, would be good. But to be great would require more. Would he do them all at once? Or one at a time?

Something for him to think about.

When Charlie snapped out of his daydream, he realized Bill had noticed his distraction.

"Sorry," Charlie said. "I was just thinking about the right pace and scope of the changes I want to lead with my team."

Bill smiled and said, "That's the beauty and value of the questions in these steps. When you pause to consider them *before* acting, you get the answers you'll need to succeed and keep from making thoughtless mistakes, which keeps you from struggling or failing once you make the change.

"I have to think some more about the scope, but I already know the proper pace," said Charlie. "What's next?"

"There's another important part to Step #4," said Bill. "And it's a good idea to do this *before* you make the change."

Now Charlie was puzzled. "Wait," he said, reciting the four simple steps. "I've decided to change, worked with my team and others to look for options and risks, created my checklist to signal the change, and I'm about to make the change. What's left????" he asked.

Bill paused for a second and said, "Once you start to change lanes, you need to finish the change and *sustain* the new course and pace toward your goal. Starting is easy. But it's finishing that counts!"

"Starting is easy...
It's finishing that counts!"

"Of course," Charlie thought. He felt so prepared and excited to start that he had hardly thought about what it would take for him or his team to *keep* operating at a higher level, let alone to continue improving and achieve their full potential.

On the one hand, he thought it would actually be easier, with more energy and confidence brimming from him and the team. But he knew that wouldn't happen indefinitely on its own. Just like traffic in a new lane could eventually slow down. New challenges and old habits could certainly slow him and the team back to where they were now.

"Turning into a new lane is just the beginning," Bill added. "Now you'll need to do what it takes to adjust the pace and *sustain* it to achieve your goals and objectives.

"In traffic, have you ever had someone pull in front of you from a slower lane, but not speed up? They just stay at the same pace, blocking *your* progress and everyone behind you? It's frustrating.

"Your team and stakeholders will be equally frustrated if your change doesn't lead to sustained progress."

"It happens all the time!" exclaimed Charlie. "Like, every day and every drive!" he added.

"And it happens just as often with changes in business, even after planning. Business leaders start with good intentions. They announce a new direction, but don't do what it takes to maintain the focus and succeed with change in their new lane. When the intended improvements don't happen as planned, or have a lasting benefit, the team, customers, and stakeholders lose enthusiasm and confidence."

Bill offered another analogy. "Think of it like follow-through in sports. Imagine golf or baseball without follow-through. Would the ball ever reach the green or clear the outfield fence? It would be pretty hard to score, let alone keep any fans interested in the game."

Then he added, "The last part of Step #4 is planning to follow through and finish what you start. Describe what the change will look and feel like when it's complete. Trust me when I tell you how useful and powerful that exercise will be when it comes to offering motivation and inspiration for you and your team to succeed all the way and achieve your goal. Change gets noticed. It energizes some and spooks others. Continue to fuel the change by sharing updates, enthusiasm, encouragement, and appreciation until the new pace and course become the norm."

"Sounds like great advice!" said Charlie. "What's next?"

"The moment you've been waiting for!" exclaimed Bill. "All of your forethought and preparation has led to this:

"It's time to change lanes. Turn the wheel. Change course. Step on the gas and show your commitment to the new direction. You and your team should *feel* the difference. The exhilaration of accelerating on a better course. Or the relief of slowing from stressful chaos to manageable focus.

"Remember, changing lanes doesn't always mean moving faster. Your change may be to pump the brakes, slow down, and give your team the time and resources necessary to succeed *reliably* at a proper pace for the new lane. Sometimes that's the best next step for a company in distress.

"In either situation, it's imperative for a leader to be visible when implementing change.

"It's imperative for a leader to be visible, when implementing change."

You want to show confidence, offer encouragement and appreciation, and inspire your team by reminding them of upcoming milestones and the 'why' behind the move. Often. *All* of the things that the four steps of changing lanes has prepared you for... I can't emphasize this enough!" Bill said emphatically.

"Got it," Charlie said, sitting up a little straighter and underlining the notes he'd been taking while Bill was talking. He knew he was not only up to the task but increasingly excited to get started.

"I can do that," He thought, then added out loud., "I can't wait to get started!"

"And you should." said Bill.

"Here's a final worksheet to help you succeed with Step #4. Consider it your 'Changing Lanes Roadmap,'" Bill said as he slid the worksheet for Step #4: Make the Change to Charlie. "There are really only three sections to fill in, but I find them immensely helpful, even after using it so many times."

"You mean *you* use these too?" asked Charlie, thinking they were something Bill had created just to help others.

"I wouldn't lead a change without them!" said Bill. "If something works, stick with it."

"Remember," he added, "relying on executive instinct, *even mine*, is nowhere near as reliable or effective as using the worksheets and following these four simple steps. Especially this last one. It's one of three big reasons why change efforts struggle or fail in business."

"Remind me again what they are?" Charlie asked, pen in hand. He knew this would be useful for the rest of his career.

"Simple." Bill said, unfolding three fingers as he listed them off.

"Number 1: Not deciding to change, due to blind spots, uncertainty, or lack of confidence.

Number 2: Poor signaling, failing to inform and involve others to gain buy-in. And,

Number 3: Not finishing. Not having the plan, commitment, or discipline to follow through to completion."

Bill then summed up. "The biggest reason of all is that most business leaders just don't *have* a simple and reliable approach to succeed with change."

"Most business leaders just don't have a simple and reliable approach to succeed with change."

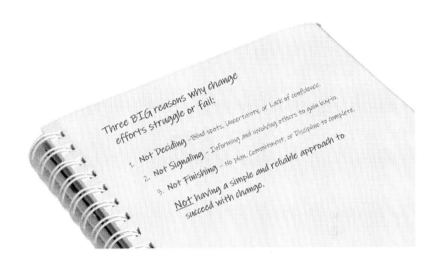

Three BIG reasons why change efforts struggle or fail:

1. Not Deciding – Blind spots, Uncertainty, or Lack of confidence.
2. Not Signaling – Informing and involving others to gain buy-in.
3. Not Finishing – No Plan, Commitment, or Discipline to complete.

Not having a simple and reliable approach to succeed with change.

He added, "If the change you want to make is important, and I sense yours is, why start if you don't 'plan' to finish? And why would you choose to wing it when there's a simple approach that works every time?"

They had both managed to finish their lunches during the conversation, so, it was time to get back to work. For Bill, that meant making his final preparations for the board meeting. And for Charlie, it was time to follow up on some open items from the week and finish the new worksheet from Bill and prepare to make the change he had been planning.

Before they left, Charlie asked Bill how things were going with his preparation for the board meeting. Bill replied that he still had some people to touch base with, and a few things to finish, which he planned to do this afternoon and over the weekend.

Then he said, "The meeting will be all day Monday, so I'm afraid I won't be available for lunch that day."

Charlie conceded that the board meeting probably took priority over their lunch meetings. He thanked Bill again profusely for all of the time and effort he was offering to help him learn to become a better leader.

Bill just winked and said, "It's my pleasure! I told you before that you're worth it." Then he added something that took Charlie by surprise.

"There's going to be some follow-up for me Tuesday morning, but why don't we meet back here for lunch at our usual time? I'd love to see how you've done with Step #4 and your plan for Changing Lanes overall. Plus, I have two more things to share with you before I leave for home Tuesday evening."

Charlie was both stunned and delighted. He couldn't believe Bill would find even more time for him, so he quickly accepted the invitation and wished him good luck with the meeting.

On his way back to the office, he was both excited to finish the exercises for Step #4, and also really curious about what else Bill could possibly want to talk with him about. He decided that by Monday he would finalize the plan to change lanes with his team and also let Bill know he was making the change.

While he'd fallen off of it lately, Charlie had a routine he liked to do on Friday afternoons to wrap up loose ends. He used it himself, and also tried to visit with each member of his team to make sure they were clear about their priorities and weren't starting from behind the following week.

For some reason, this week, even with all the time he'd spent with Bill and doing the Changing Lanes exercises, he had nothing more important to do this afternoon than check in with his team and finish the final worksheet.

He decided to start with his biggest challenge and met separately with the two team members who always seemed to be at odds with each other. After getting their updates, he thanked them for their progress and offered his advice and assistance with their challenges. He then told them that he wanted all three of them to meet together on Monday to discuss some important new priorities.

Rather than offer any more detail, he decided he would wait until they met on Monday to explain more fully what the new priorities might be, and why they had to meet together. Charlie would be ready.

After that, he touched base with each of his top two team members and found them in good spirits, having made some welcome progress. In the back of his mind, Charlie was wondering whether the new energy and optimism he had gained from his meetings with Bill was already rubbing off on his team.

Getting a head start on his lane change, he expressed his appreciation, not only for their progress but for the example and leadership they were providing for other members of the team.

His last stop was to check in on his team member who had returned that day from sick leave. He knew she was buried, so he'd been careful to give her some uninterrupted time and not add anything new to her already long list of tasks and responsibilities.

When he stepped in, he could tell she'd "Had a week" and was still spinning several plates.

Charlie started by telling her how glad he was that she was back and asked how she was doing. After a quick update, he offered to help with a few of the contacts that were giving her a challenge, which seemed to lighten her load and her spirits. She also paused to thank Charlie for giving her the time to catch up, not putting any new workload on her, and now offering to help.

Charlie told her that he could relate, that he'd been in the same situation several times and knew what it took to get back in the game.

He told her to wrap up what she was doing and take the rest of the day off so she could be fully rested for Monday.

At first, she resisted, but then realized that Charlie's advice made sense. She smiled and conceded that she would be out within the hour.

He thanked her for working so hard to catch up and said that he was looking forward to having her back in the game next week.

"If you want your people to care for the customers and care for the mission," Charlie remembered, "you have to care for them!"

After finishing his rounds, Charlie was generally pleased with his team's progress and demeanor. Yet things felt just average. Not awful. But not awesome either. And awesome is what he wanted.

He was eager to finish the worksheet Bill had given him for Step #4 so he could start changing lanes on Monday.

He cleared his desk and opened the worksheet. Not surprisingly, it started by having him rewrite his goal, objectives, and the "why" behind the change – again. While he was tempted to just copy it from Step #2, he remembered how he'd refined it there. And Bill's explanation that each time you do this exercise, it tightens up and becomes more accurate, compelling, and easier to share.

So, he wrote it again. Sure enough, this time, it got even better.

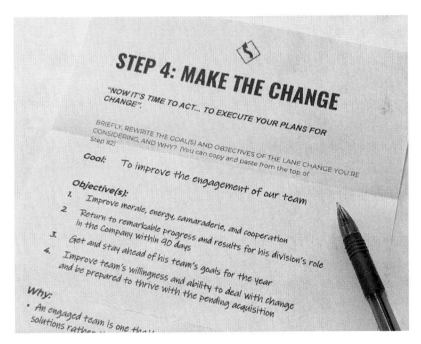

STEP 4: MAKE THE CHANGE

"NOW IT'S TIME TO ACT... TO EXECUTE YOUR PLANS FOR CHANGE".

BRIEFLY, REWRITE THE GOAL(S) AND OBJECTIVES OF THE LANE CHANGE YOU'RE CONSIDERING, AND WHY? (You can copy and paste from the top of Step #2)

Goal: To improve the engagement of our team

Objective(s):
1. Improve morale, energy, camaraderie, and cooperation
2. Return to remarkable progress and results for his division's role in the company within 90 days
3. Get and stay ahead of his team's goals for the year
4. Improve team's willingness and ability to deal with change and be prepared to thrive with the pending acquisition

Why:
- An engaged team is one that...
  solutions rather...

"That would be a significant and worthwhile lane change," thought Charlie.

The "Why?" he'd written previously was still perfect:

"An engaged team is one that's positive, confident, and focused on solutions rather than problems or workload. It will be more reliable, more productive, and more likely to succeed than one that is not."

Plus, "It's far more attractive, energizing, and fun to be a part of than one that's disengaged and focused on struggles and problems." "…Like they have been," Charlie thought again.

As he finished rewriting the "Why" behind the change, he was even *more* committed to making it happen.

After that, it looked like there were only three parts to the worksheet, just like Bill described:

- List the steps to *start* the change.
- List the steps to *finish* the change. And then…
- Change lanes.

He remembered why Bill had it broken out like this, so he started writing.

First, he decided the proper pace and scope of his change. Then he listed specific steps to implement the change, along with objectives and target dates for their completion.

Much of this he had already considered, so it was easy to fill in.

He had to admit that, normally, he would have just taken action. But this exercise helped him to be much more aware and intentional about what needed to happen, and when, in order to start the change off well.

He wanted to begin immediately and make the change as quickly as possible. But he also wanted to make the change gracefully, without any sudden disruption that would leave his team wondering what the heck was going on.

This suddenly made sense. It would keep him from moving too quickly, too slowly, or missing something that was vital to his success.

Reminding himself of what he wanted, and answers to previous questions, he wrote:

#1: Resolve the issues between the feuding team members.

Objectives:

a) Meet with the feuding team members to reconcile their differences. Request or insist on and achieve collaboration.

b) If not resolved within 1-2 weeks, decide who to replace. One, or both? He could not allow this cancer to exist in his team.

The target date for the first objective was Monday, with follow-ups on Friday and at the end of the following week. In two weeks, this issue would be fixed or in process to be eliminated.

#2: Engage the team. Continue communications to understand their needs, confirm their importance and priorities, express appreciation for their contributions, and encourage their growth.

Objectives:

a) Secure the support of the top two team members.

b) Continue the conversation with each team member on their ideas to improve, along with their ideas for solutions. For example, what would be needed to implement their improvement?

c) Confirm that they have what they need to do their job.

d) Emphasize their importance to the success of the project, and the company overall.

e) Express appreciation for their contributions and "best work."

Charlie had learned years before from a long-time mentor that one of the best ways to get people to strive for improvement and excellence was to simply ask, "Is this your best work?" While initially asking the question came across as a challenge, in many cases the answer was simply "yes." And if the answer wasn't yes, or revealed uncertainty, it created a great opportunity to discuss what *would* be their best work, and how they could do it.

The target date for Step #2 was the coming week. But Charlie also realized that this process should be ongoing, not to become tiresome, but often enough that each member of the team would know that:

- Their ideas for improvement, and especially solutions, were always welcome.
- Charlie wanted to make sure they had what they needed to succeed.
- They were important to the success of the team and company.
- He appreciated their reliability and contributions to the team and project.

#3: Improve team communication, spirit, energy, and ongoing collaboration.

In addition to working with team members individually, Charlie planned to bring a new approach and energy to his weekly team meetings. Most people loathed meetings, but Charlie knew that done right, meetings were essential to exchange information, ensure collaboration, provide training, brainstorm solutions, and infuse energy. It was hard to infuse energy with email and virtual meetings.

While he knew those things, he had to admit that his team meetings had become something the team felt they *had* to attend. He didn't want meetings to be an endurance test, but rather a reliable opportunity to improve everyone's understanding and abilities and to ensure success.

The turnaround here was on him. He listed the objectives for this step:

a) Establish expectations for the meetings and circulate an agenda at least one day prior to every meeting, helping team members know what to expect and come prepared to learn and contribute.

b) Share the ideas for improvement that team members had offered, and his motives for asking.

c) Emphasize that he believed in the team, and that wanted to see them each:

    a. Return to making remarkable progress and delivering results for the division.

    b. Get and stay ahead of their goals for the year. And

    c. Improve their ability and willingness to deal with change.

The target date for launching the first two was the coming week, while he would share the third objective the following week.

Within two to three weeks, they would be moving into a new lane, with new energy and accelerating progress.

He also wanted to take Bill up on his offer to visit and share his perspective with the team, thinking that would help to launch the lane change. So, he listed that as well.

#4: Invite others to meet with the team periodically to share outside perspectives and offer insights that would help the team to understand their priorities.

His objectives for this step were:

a) Include the president, board members, other senior leaders, customers, and vendors. And,

b) Create opportunities for these guests to express their appreciation and the importance of his team's work.

While he'd written more than he had expected, he realized that just thoughtfully filling in this section had given him a perfect roadmap and steps to follow to *start* this important change.

Next, was "List the steps to finish – to sustain the new course and pace toward the goal." If the steps to finish were as revealing as the steps to start, Charlie wanted to map them out.

The worksheet said: "List some checkpoints and milestones you'll use to confirm for yourself and others that the change is working."

After just a minute, he realized that some of the checkpoints and milestones for his goals would be objectives, and listed them:

1. Feud between team members resolved and replaced with respect and collaboration.

2. Team members routinely offer ideas and implement solutions to improve progress.

3. Team getting and staying ahead of goals throughout the year.

4. Helpful agendas - sent at least 24 hours before *every* team meeting.

5. Inspiring, insightful guests, visiting and contributing to team's awareness and sense of meaning twice monthly.

He also listed two subjective ones:

6. Visible improvement in team's energy, confidence, and collaboration, to deliver their best work and achieve goals on, or ahead of, schedule.

7. An emerging awareness of their importance, and a sense of pride in the contributions they were making, for the company and customers.

The third part of Step #4 offered inspiration and encouragement to take action, to change lanes, with tips on how to succeed. It read:

"All of your forethought and preparation has led to this... It's time to turn the wheel. To change course. To step on the gas and add energy to the new direction.

You and your team should feel the exhilaration of accelerating onto a better course.

For a leader, it is imperative to be visible when implementing change.

Exhibit confidence, offer encouragement, and inspire your team by reminding them of the milestone targets and the "why" behind the move.

The importance of this step cannot be overstated.

Check items off the items you've listed in above to start and finish your Lane Change – as planned – and communicate progress to your team and stakeholders both."

"Good advice! thought Charlie.

He sat back for a minute and realized just how far he had come in just a week, from feeling frustrated and disappointed with his team's languishing energy and performance to having a plan and specific objectives that he was confident they could achieve together.

The finishing exercise for making the change was to "**Imagine the Future**: *Describe your ideal outcome, or the transformation that happens with your business or project as a result of succeeding with this change.*"

This left Charlie puzzled but intrigued, so he let his mind drift into the future and imagine what life would be like in the new lane. It was both fun and inspiring. He wrote:

✓ *"It's three months from the day we started to change lanes and the transformation has been remarkable.*

✓ *My team and I are operating with newfound energy, confidence, and the capacity to handle whatever comes our way.*

✓ *Productivity has surged as we moved from uncertainty and struggle to clarity and confidence, handling our roles in the acquisition with ease."*

While not part of his original vision, Charlie added one final remark. *"We are setting a positive example and assisting other teams in the company with our new approach for changing lanes."*

He had no idea how accurate his description would become...

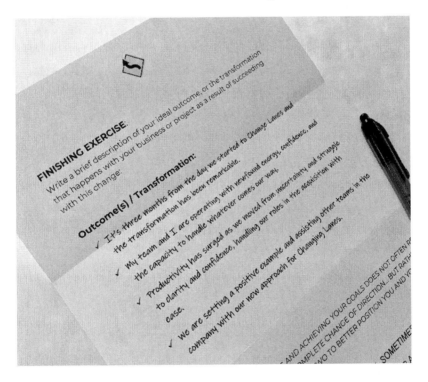

"That was energizing!" thought Charlie as he scanned his answers to the questions for **Step #4: MAKE the Change**. While he wouldn't have normally gone this far, listing specific steps to start and finish a change he intended to lead, he marveled at the clarity and confidence the changing lanes approach had helped him to achieve.

With just a few thoughtful minutes per step, he had a solid plan and the determination to see it through.

He packed up his worksheets and was already looking forward to Monday when he would put his plan into action.

On the drive home, he couldn't help but see the rhythm and simplicity of the changing lanes approach: Decide. Look. Signal. Change. He must have changed lanes a dozen times or more along the way, always to do better, to avoid slowdowns, to improve progress, and to arrive at his destination, on time or ahead of time.

"Business really *is* like driving," Charlie thought.

Rather than having challenges from work and unfinished projects weighing on his mind, knowing his priorities, and having such a clear plan for the following week allowed Charlie to give his full focus to his family over the weekend.

At dinner that night, each member of the family shared not only what they did and learned that day, but also their best experience of the week.

When it was Charlie's turn, his win for the day was answering the questions for Step #4, creating a roadmap to start and finish the lane change with his team. For the week, he reflected on learning the simple changing lanes approach in just a few days, thanks to Bill, and on how determined he was to get started the following week.

Even the kids commented that they noticed their father's renewed energy as the week went on.

Between the kid's sports activities, chores around the house, and a few social get-togethers with neighbors and friends, the weekend flew by.

THE APPLICATION

Changing Lanes

Chapter 8

READY, SET, GO!

On Monday morning, Charlie was up early. He was excited, not just to get started with his team, but also to see how the board meeting would turn out as they deliberated the acquisition.

On the way in, he picked his way through traffic, thinking about the best timing and approach to get his team on board with the lane change.

Once, as he was lost in thought, he found himself stuck in a lane that was slowing him down. He was determined not to let that happen on the job, and instead, to remain focused on his goal to energize the team.

At the office, he started by reviewing his priorities. On Mondays, that meant visiting each member of his team to make sure they had clear direction and what they needed to succeed for the week. Today he would include the first steps of his plan to eliminate problems and accelerate progress.

After reviewing his team's project plans, he sent and replied to important emails and other communication channels, then headed out to meet with his feuding team members.

When he arrived at the conference room where the meeting was scheduled, they had both arrived. Promptness and reliability were not their issues. There was a feeling of uncertainty and unease in the air, which Charlie had anticipated.

He started pleasantly, thanking them both for showing up and then complimented each, listing the specific strengths and talent they brought to the team. As he expressed his appreciation, he sensed the mood in the room switch to bewilderment. So, he cut to the chase.

"It's no secret that you two don't see eye-to-eye. And while I'm not sure if it's disagreement or disrespect, it diminishes the value of your contributions and slows us down as a team."

He went on to cite a few recent examples of how their dissent had held up their ability to produce, and how it even cast a shadow on the spirit and productivity of the team.

Now, both were obviously feeling uncomfortable. Charlie was sure that they didn't like being "outed." And they didn't like the notion that they could be hindering the team's success.

He continued, "While I'd like to understand the problem, what I *really* want – what we *need* for the good of the team – is to have it resolved and have you two working together to reliably *accelerate* our progress.

"Help me understand the issue. Or issues," Charlie added, "if there *is* more than one."

He asked each to be open and candid, sharing what and why they showed such disregard for one another.

He assured them that he had no problem with disagreement, and in fact, found value in it, but that there was *no* room for disrespect or disregard. While things were awkward for a moment, Charlie knew this was a step that had to be taken if these two were ever going to come together.

While the conversation began cautiously, and neither admitted it outright, after a few exchanges, what revealed itself was a thinly disguised competition. They each wanted to be the smartest member of the team, and not be upstaged, outdone, or outwitted by the other.

Believing he had uncovered the root issue; Charlie paused the conversation with a smile and called it out.

"You are both incredibly talented, with a gift for finding and implementing solutions," he said, "And I believe we have only begun to see the value you can bring to the team."

"When you clash, it causes consternation that slows us down. If you collaborate, it speeds us up. There's a reason you're both on this team. If you were both the same, one of you would not be necessary," he said, then paused for effect.

"But there is *strength* in differences! And that's what I want to see."

Charlie jumped up to the whiteboard and grabbed a marker, which startled them both.

"One plus one *should* equal two, right?" They both shrugged and nodded as he wrote: **1 + 1 = 2**

"But that's not what we're getting." Keeping it about the team, as he threw a slash across the equals sign" **1 + 1 ≠ 2**

"Here's what's really happening," he said and wrote **1 vs. 1 = 0**

Circling the zero several times for effect, he said "When you two feud, even covertly, it creates tangible and unnecessary tension that slows us all down. The team feels they have to "pick a camp," and I typically have to find a way to reconcile your differences, all of which burns time and energy."

"Here's what I *see*," Charlie said as he turned back to the board and wrote **1 + 1 = ____**. The sum of the equation was left blank.

He faced them again and said, "Individually, you are both very good at what you do," Charlie said paying them a solid compliment. "But *together*, you're better. You can even be *great!*" he said as he spun back to the board and finished the equation with a giant **3**.

"That's what I want!" Charlie exclaimed. "That's what the *team* needs." He added, "Together, you are a force multiplier." He turned back and emphasized the **3** a few more times to help drive home the point. They sat in silence for a moment, letting that sink in.

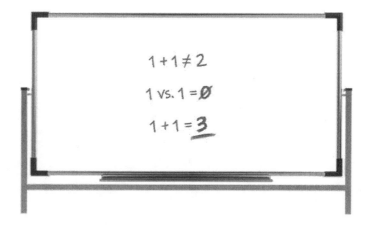

A small but silent nod of potential acknowledgment came from each of them.

Charlie cited a few examples of how the experience and strengths of one could be compounded by the strengths of the other.

Then he added a question that brought the point home. "If you had two all-pro players on your team, which you two potentially are, would you want them *competing* with each other to be the most valuable player, with a 'me-first' attitude?

"Or would you want them *combining* their strengths to win games? To build a winning culture with a 'team-first' attitude?"

It was a leading question, but they both acknowledged that they'd want the latter outcome.

"So… how can we get there from here?" Charlie continued.

"Neither one of you needs to *change*," Charlie said, pausing again and drawing looks of both relief and bewilderment. "I wouldn't trade your strengths for the world."

"We just need you to change lanes with your attitude toward each other," he said, drawing directly on the approach he'd learned from Bill. He then added, "We need you to go from independence, disregard, and competition to respect, willingness, and enthusiastic collaboration. To help each other excel…

"Working *together* to come up with solutions and improvements will help us *all* to win. If you can do that, you will both grow from good to great!" Charlie finished. "I need to know that you're both on board… that you're willing to do this."

They were both nodding now, less grudgingly than before. Charlies guessed that "changing lanes" was an easier concept to consider than if he had told them *they* had to change, which would have been his normal approach.

The tension had dissipated a bit but was now replaced with uncertainty and curiosity. "Where do we start?" one team member asked, with an apparent willingness to consider a new lane.

"I'm glad you asked!" Charlie smiled again as he turned to face them both. "There may be some big new challenges and opportunities coming soon for our team. I'm not at liberty yet to discuss it, and frankly, I don't know the full extent or details myself, but we'll all know in the coming weeks. And I want our team to be ready. I'm asking everyone to share how we can improve. What do *they* see that we can do better? And what solutions can we implement to make it happen?"

"I'll be talking with each of them next, but I wanted to start with the two of you, because frankly, gaining your collaboration is my *top priority* for improving the team." He let that sink in.

"While the others will be working individually – I want their unique perspectives – I want the two of you to work *together*. I want you to share your perspectives with one another, in advance, and combine forces to distill the most important things that you see for us to improve, along with potential solutions we can implement."

"Show me, and show yourselves that 1+1 equals *at least* 3… and maybe more?!"

Charlie knew that one of the best ways to build rapport between people with differences was to have them do a project or solve a problem together.

He began to see their acceptance. They could see how serious and determined Charlie was. If it was *his* top priority, that made it theirs. They both realized that this wasn't a scolding or formal counseling session, but a call to action. A challenge.

Charlie summed up by saying, "I want you two to put your heads together, share perspectives, and come back to me by 10 a.m. Thursday with your consensus on what we need, or what we can do to improve our performance as a team. Remember," Charlie said as he stood, pointing at the whiteboard, "1 + 1 = *at least* 3."

"I believe in you!" he added. "Together, you are a force. Can I count on your collaboration?"

They both agreed, nodding as they stood. He shook their hands, thanked them for coming, and said he appreciated their willingness to work together. As they left the room, he looked them both in the eye and said, "I want to see your *best* work."

He watched them talking, already exchanging ideas and plans as they walked away. While he knew this was far from fixed, he marveled at the difference just a few minutes of thoughtful communication could make.

"That went fairly well…" Charlie thought, wondering why he hadn't taken action sooner. In an instant, he knew the answer: because while he wasn't happy with their ongoing friction, he had never actually decided to address it. Until now.

He took a few minutes to document the meeting, listing both the issues discussed and the desired behavior. Then sent it to HR for their file(s). Either as a basis for a future recommendation, or a first step for any additional corrective action.

Bill was right. He could see why "not deciding" was one of the main reasons why important changes fail to happen in business.

Charlie was done tolerating anything less than excellence. Especially from himself.

It was time to visit the rest of his team. As each thought it was their usual Monday visit with Charlie, they worked through the compulsory topics about project status, priorities, and any needs they had for the week. Charlie then returned to the question he'd floated with each person previously, requesting their thoughts and ideas on how they and the team could improve.

This time, he let them know that he wanted to measurably improve the team's performance and progress and wanted to start by collecting each of their perspectives. Not just on what to improve, but also on solutions. How could the team best accomplish the changes they would be recommending?

Some already had ideas, which they discussed. Others hadn't yet given it much thought. Charlie emphasized that he was looking for input from everyone and asked them to send him their thoughts by noon on Thursday. He added that they would have a team meeting at 10 a.m. Friday morning to discuss everyone's recommendations as a group.

"Remember," he closed each visit by saying, "problems, ideas, and solutions," setting the stage for them to be solution-oriented and adding how much he valued their perspective and was looking forward to seeing their "best work."

He finished in time for lunch and headed to the coffee shop alone, reflecting on each of the meetings he'd just had. He wasn't sure if it was just his imagination, but he detected he was releasing some new energy from his team. Their sense that things were about to change for the better, and that they would have a hand in it, was already building support and enthusiasm for improving the team's performance.

As he ate, his thoughts shifted to the board meeting, wondering how it was going? Whether the acquisition would be approved, and what that might mean for his team.

They would be ready, Charlie thought firmly, determined to improve their performance, regardless of the board meeting outcome.

He was already looking forward to lunch with Bill tomorrow, not just to learn the outcome of the board meeting, but also to share that he was already deep into Step #3 for changing lanes with his team. He was also eager to learn about what else Bill had hinted at.

Having met with each member of his team and getting their updates on priorities and progress planned for the week, Charlie finished eating and went back to his office to handle more communication and prepare the resources necessary to help his team succeed.

On the way home that afternoon, he recalled the steps of changing lanes and his commitment. He had made the decision to energize his team and significantly improve their performance in the next 90 days.

With his request for their input, he would be getting their help with **Step #2: to Look for Options and Risks.** And **Step #3: Signal the Change** with each team member individually. This Friday he would hold the team meeting, where he would get more specific about options and plans for the team to change lanes.

He decided that tomorrow, he would assemble *his* thoughts on problems, opportunities, and solutions as well. Then compare what he saw with what the team offered and be ready to add any items that he thought may be missing.

That evening at dinner, the family again noticed Charlie's enthusiasm and energy. Without going into detail, he shared his plan to change lanes and described the meetings he'd had today to start the process, adding that he would know how well it was going when he got their recommendations on Thursday and held the meeting on Friday.

On Tuesday morning Charlie was eager to get to the office. He felt relieved and energized by the challenge of improving his team's energy and performance. "Just like driving!" he thought, comparing the feeling to the relief and energy that happened when he escaped being stuck in traffic, changing into a new lane and accelerating to the pace he wanted.

He was ready, not just to manage the projects he had in progress, but to work on his *own* ideas to improve the team.

And most of all, to catch up with Bill. He wanted to hear about the board meeting, and also to share the start of his lane change with the team. He sent Bill a text to confirm and got an immediate reply. Bill was looking forward to lunch as well. They agreed to meet a few minutes early to beat the rush.

Before he knew it, it was nearing time for lunch, so he headed down to the coffee shop. Today was his treat. In addition to his own lunch, he picked out what he'd seen were Bill's favorites and had everything on their table when Bill arrived.

Charlie walked over to greet him and let him know that lunch was "on him," and how much he was looking forward to meeting with him again today.

"I've been looking forward to it too," Bill said. Then explained that he had a flight back home and had to be on his way to the airport early that afternoon. So, Charlie's treat had made Bill's day easier, and also bought them some extra time.

They both settled in, and Charlie started the conversation, "I've signaled my team and started our lane change!" he said enthusiastically. After finishing Step #4 on Friday afternoon, I didn't see any reason to hesitate."

Bill was smiling now. "Knowing what you're planning, I don't see *any* reason to hesitate. Tell me, how's it going?" Bill asked.

Charlie explained how he'd started with his biggest issue, the one thing he thought would make the biggest difference, at least from his perspective. "I met yesterday with my two feuding team members, not just to understand and quell their disputes, but to gain their collaboration."

"That's a big shift," Bill said. "What did you do and how did it go?"

Charlie said, "I started by letting them know how talented and potentially valuable they both were to me and the team, yet how their antagonism toward each other was actually putting a drag on our progress and culture. I explained that if they would collaborate instead, the whole team would see a compound effect – much greater than what either of them could contribute on their own."

"Did they get it?" asked Bill.

"They seemed to," said Charlie. "I didn't want to wait for that to happen on its own, so I put them on a project together immediately."

"What are you having them do?" Bill asked.

"Help with our lane change," Charlie grinned. "I asked them to put their heads together and get back to me by Thursday with their best ideas to help improve the team's morale and productivity."

"That's brilliant," said Bill.

Charlie replied, "They both seemed agreeable. Not quite enthusiastic, but I'm cautiously optimistic that they will change lanes for the better and help us make progress." Then he added, "If they don't, I'll have different choices to make. I'm not going to tolerate dissent and antagonism on this team."

Bill chimed in, "Sadly, we don't get what we want in business. We get what we tolerate. So, you're definitely on the right track." Then he asked, "What about the rest of your team?"

Charlie explained how he'd met with each of them individually with the same request: for them to forward, by Thursday, their ideas on what they or the team could do to improve, along with solutions. "I'm trying to develop problem solvers, not just problem spotters," he said.

"I used the roadmap from Step #4 to plan the start and the finish of our change, he continued. "When I had to 'imagine the future' and describe what things would be like in three months, well, that *really* inspired me to make it happen."

Bill said, "That's a great start! Not only are you signaling your intent for the team to change lanes to improve their energy and productivity, but you're *involving* them by getting their input and letting them be part of the solution. Those are *both* key to minimizing resistance and building support."

"I've had a great teacher!" exclaimed Charlie. I'm looking forward to the next two weeks and the transformation that will happen in the following months.

Then he said, "Tell me about the Bonus Step. If we use the four steps to change lanes whenever we need improvement or progress, what else is left to do?"

Chapter 9

THE QUIZ

B ill replied, "The four steps *do* work, Charlie. *Any* time you need to lead successful change. But there is the fifth step that, frankly, you've already started."

"I'm really not surprised," Bill added. "It's optional. It's not required to lead successful change, but once you know how and why it works, I doubt you'll want to operate without it."

Charlie looked puzzled and he asked, "What do you mean, I've already started?"

Bill went in a different direction with a question of his own. "When you drive anywhere, how many times do you change lanes?"

Now Charlie was *really* puzzled.

"I don't know," he said. "It depends…"

"On what?" Bill asked.

Charlie thought for a second and said, "How far I'm going."

Bill nodded, saying, "And…" egging Charlie on to continue.

"Traffic," he answered.

"What do you mean by traffic?" Bill asked quickly.

Charlie was beginning to feel that this was a test. Or some sort of quiz. "I mean, whether it's moving at a reasonable speed." He added, "Is it flowing at the pace it should, or is the lane I'm in bogging down, going slower than it should." "

So, let me ask you again," said Bill, "When you drive anywhere, how many times do you change lanes?"

Charlie replied, "As often as I need to reach my destination on time."

"Do you wait until you're going slow or boxed-in to start changing lanes?" Bill asked, suddenly full of questions.

Charlie replied quickly, "Not if I can help it. Once I'm making good time, I try to keep it up."

"So, how do you 'help it'?" Bill asked, pulling his question from Charlie's reply.

Charlie knew Bill wasn't toying with him. There had to be a lesson here somewhere… What did he mean when he had said, "Not if I can help it"? Then, it dawned on him. He answered, "I help it by paying attention!" Charlie said.

"To what?" Bill quickly asked.

They were both smiling now. The point of the quiz was becoming clear. And Charlie knew the answers as the pace picked-up.

"To the traffic." Charlie said.

"Where?" Bill asked.

"In front of me." Charlie replied.

"Just in your lane?" Bill asked.

"No," Charlie replied. I watch all of the lanes.

"For what?" Bill asked.

"For brake lights and congestion. For which lanes are moving and which are bogging down." Charlie said.

"Brake lights? Bill asked.

"Yes, I can often see way ahead that the lane I'm in or some other lane is slowing down by watching for brake lights ahead." Charlie answered.

"So, just by watching the traffic ahead, you can keep from getting boxed in and bogged down?" Bill quizzed, picking up and looking at his phone, which was unusual.

Then Charlie got the hint. "No," he replied. "If I have it on, my navigation app can warn me about slow-downs and even recommend alternate routes to my destination."

Before he could fire another question, Charlie said, "I also watch what's going on alongside. On *both* sides." Then added, "Behind me too, using my mirrors!"

"Why?" asked Bill.

"So I know what my options are if I need to changes lanes to keep my pace, to speed things up, or take a detour," Charlie replied.

"And if things slow down and you decide to change lanes, what do you do?" Bill asked.

"I follow the four steps! Charlie replied, thinking back to the days of their first meetings when he was relearning the steps he used when driving. "Decide, look, signal, and change."

Bill sat back, smiling.

Charlie sensed the quiz was over and the priceless lesson would soon be apparent.

Chapter 10

BONUS STEP: ACCELERATE!

Bill said "Charlie, you've just described what happens in the Bonus Step. You remain vigilant, looking for things that will slow you down. Your team, vendors, customers, and other resources you have are your navigation app. They reveal issues you can't see from your perspective. You also have them look for *opportunities* and options to sustain or accelerate progress. And you do this routinely, so when there's a need to change, or opportunity to improve, you and your team are ready to go."

"The funny part is," Bill added "all this vigilance takes *less* energy than waiting to get bogged down and having to recover yet again from lost momentum and missed goals. In fact, the exercise energizes your team and creates an organization that quickly becomes a market leader."

"How so?" Charlie asked.

"Imagine three companies," Bill said, continuing, "All three are the same size, in the same industry and geography, with the same talent.

"Company #1 has no simple or reliable approach to leading successful change. When the need for change arises, the leaders do their best, but wing it. Relying on instinct, experience, and whatever resources they can muster to react, recover, and somehow stay in the game. Over time, they will predictably fall behind."

"Company #2 knows and uses the changing lanes approach. Whenever a challenge appears to slow them down, or an opportunity to improve arises, they use the four simple steps to succeed with change and get back in the game. They are resilient and reliably successful."

"Company #3 knows and uses the changing lanes approach too, but also makes the Bonus Step into a tradition, routinely *looking* for problems to overcome, or opportunities to seize to accelerate progress. Because of their vigilance, initiative, and conditioning, this company soon becomes a market leader and is very hard to beat."

"Which one would you rather be a part of?" Bill asked.

"That's easy," said Charlie. "Clearly #3."

"Well, it's your choice!" Bill declared.

"*My* choice?" Charlie asked, wondering how a strategic decision like that could be his.

Bill said, "the Bonus Step is called Accelerate, because you and your team are *always* looking for ways to improve."

"But, aside from my little quiz, I'm afraid I don't have much to teach you on that."

Charlie was concerned and asked, "Why is that?"

Bill replied, "Because you've already made the choice. You're already doing it! I told you your instincts were good.

"The exercise you have your team doing right now, to bring their observations about problems and opportunities, and ideas for solutions on how to improve… That is *most* of it. All that's left is having a rhythm for the exercise, and process to select which recommendations to act on, when to move, and whom to put in charge. *Done right, there is not a better way to accelerate the progress of any business*," Bill added, with emphasis.

Charlie could see that he had accidentally *started* his lane change with the exercise from the Bonus Step. "Is it really this easy?" he asked. "Just four simple steps to accelerate progress and succeed with change? And one more to become a market leader?" he added.

"It is," Bill replied. "Like I said when we met last week, people make too much of change. They almost automatically think and say things like 'Change is hard,' expecting resistance, hardship, and difficulty."

He continued, "What they're really saying is that they don't know how to do it *well*. They're uncertain of success. Or maybe they even anticipate failure. Anything seems hard until you know how to do it."

"When people say that 'Change is Hard,' What they're really saying is that they don't know how to do it *well*."

Bill added. "There are many published approaches to leading and managing change. "But I've found that simple solutions work best.

Bill emphasized, "Once business leaders realize that every solution or improvement requires change, and that there are just four simple steps they can take to succeed, there's no stopping them, especially when those four simple steps are the same as something they already know how to do!"

Charlie nodded as he let that sink in. He couldn't see *any* reason why the plan he'd drafted with Bill's four steps for changing lanes wouldn't work. He knew there would be challenges. He also knew that a plan was just a reference point for future change. But having made the decision and commitment to change, having looked at the options and risks, signaling and involving anyone affected, and having specific steps and dates to start and finish, his lane change would transform the team to fit his vision of the future and allow them to achieve their full potential.

He wrote **"SIMPLE is BEST!"** in his notebook, then underlined it and decided to use it as a mantra with his team going forward.

Chapter 11

THE ACQUISITION

As he finished his thought, he turned back to Bill and said, "I should have asked this first… How did the board meeting go yesterday?"

Bill replied, "We had some *great* discussion into the afternoon, and in the end, voted unanimously to move ahead with the acquisition."

He quickly added, "It was really due to Liz's insight and the work she did to involve the board, getting their input early, and communicating the risks and benefits of moving on it now."

"This is confidential, of course," Bill added, "so please keep it to yourself until Liz and the PR team make the announcements."

Charlie assured him that he would, then asked, "So, what does this mean for you? How active will you be in the acquisition and merging the cultures?"

Bill said, "Well, you'll be seeing a bit more of me, at least for a while."

Charlie smiled wide and said, "That's fine by me!"

Bill explained that the terms of the acquisition expanded the board, adding two seats for leaders from the company they acquired.

"Liz has asked me to mentor them through their first year, so, I'll be doing some pre-work, getting them up to speed on our goals and priorities. To share our best practices and see what practices *they* have that can help the whole enterprise."

"That sounds important," Charlie observed. "It is," Bill replied. "That's why I like to do it in person."

Bill added, "Any time you're leading a transformation, you want to be present. Helping these new board members to be informed, valued, and comfortable is vital if we want them to contribute and make the difference we're counting on.

"Being in position to see their world and our operation through their eyes, to address their questions and concerns, and most of all, to get their recommendations and support, is key if we want to maximize the benefits and value of making the acquisition."

"Sounds like great advice!" Charlie noted.

Chapter 12

THE CHALLENGE

Bill said, "That's not all..." He paused for a moment, then looked at Charlie and said, "I've told Liz a bit about our conversations and your plans to elevate your team. She knows we're having this conversation today."

"It's going to take more than *my* presence and *my* work with these two board members to ensure the success of this acquisition. It's going to take a regular presence here, at the front line."

Then Bill caught Charlie by surprise, "I'd like your help. I've recommended to Liz and the board that you and your team take the lead with onboarding the new teams and helping them to fit in and be productive as soon as possible."

Charlie nearly choked on his lunch. He was stunned! After a long pause, he stammered, "But, but Bill... I'm not sure I'm ready for that! My team isn't ready for that. We've hardly begun our own lane change. How can we possibly coordinate lane changes for the rest of the company?!"

Bill grinned and said, "I told you; you have great instincts. And now you have a simple way to succeed. The way you've embraced and applied the changing lanes approach will not only work with *your* team. It is *exactly* what it will take to bring these two companies together."

"Besides," he added, "You never learn anything like when you teach it. The best way for you and your team to rise to the next level is to use and share this approach with teams on both sides. Coming out of it, we'll have one big solution-oriented team that not only doesn't resist change but goes *looking* for it on a regular basis to make us a market leader."

He continued, "I know you're just getting started with your own lane change. And you can say no, of course. But why don't you put your plan into action for the next two weeks and we'll continue the conversation when I return."

Bill added, "I know that part of your plan was to have senior leaders visit with your team, so if my schedule works for you, put me on the agenda for the week I return. I'd be delighted to support the improvements you're making however I can."

Charlie sat in stunned silence. He had two weeks to make his lane change and was now staring at the possibility of an even *bigger* one. His brain was going a mile a minute.

Finally, he said to Bill, "Okay. Let me see how far I get with my team in the next two weeks. Regardless of that, I want you to visit with my team at our meeting." They both pulled out their calendars to confirm an agreeable day and time.

Charlie said, "I'll let you know when you return if I think we'll be ready for the bigger challenge. If it works for you, let's meet for dinner the evening you arrive. My treat!" Charlie added. "I certainly owe you for all of the time and guidance you've offered me at a time when I really needed it."

"You don't owe me a thing." said Bill. "Like I said, You're worth it! I enjoy helping people to be and do their best. It's what I enjoy most about leadership and business."

He added. "But I'm certainly not going to turn down a dinner invitation… Let's plan on it. I'll send my arrival plans when I have them and you can let me know where and when we'll meet."

As they finished up, Charlie bid farewell to Bill when he left to catch his flight.

Chapter 13

PREPARATION

Charlie headed back to his office, still reeling at the thought of his team playing a lead role in the acquisition. "We're going to need plenty of energy and be at our best to pull this off," he thought. "Better get going with the transformation I've planned."

When he got back to his desk, he made a few notes about some of the things that he thought would be helpful, and even essential, for his team to build confidence and be at their best, ASAP. He wondered what the team would turn in and whether they would see the same priorities.

He sent an individual email to each member of his team, reminding them to have their recommendations for changes and solutions to him by midday Thursday, and added a personal note to each team member letting them know how much he valued their perspective and contributions.

This was going to be a pivotal moment for them all. He didn't want anyone disappearing into the group, taking it lightly, or treating it like "one more thing" they had to do to finish their list.

That meant *he* had to treat it with equal importance.

He cleared his schedule for Thursday afternoon, giving himself time to review and organize the change recommendations his team would submit, then started thinking about how he would run the team meeting on Friday.

His plan quickly came together. He made some shorthand notes, which were all he would use when the team eventually got together.

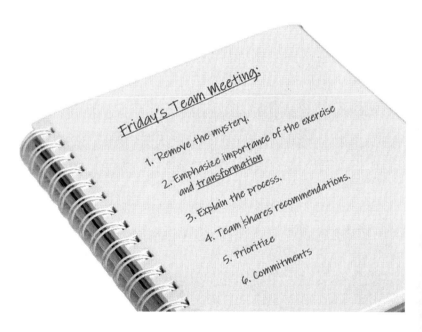

His plan was to come out of the meeting Friday with understanding, trust, shared priorities, determination, and a high level of commitment to ensure that the agreed changes would be implemented successfully.

Wednesday came and went quickly. He sensed that there was a new level of vigor and determination flowing through the team. Work always seemed to go more quickly with hope and purpose. As he made his rounds with the team, he asked how they were doing with their recommendations to improve. Several shared what they were proposing, to validate their perspectives.

He took extra time with each of the two feuding team members he'd had met with on Monday morning. He wanted to get their individual perspectives on how things were going.

He'd seen them together several times since their Monday meeting but detected more reluctance to collaborate from one than the other. He shared his observation, and as they talked it out, it became apparent that the issue was 'mindreading'… A term Charlie had learned to use when one person assumes that they know another person's motives, thought and intentions. As in this case, it was often a blind spot. One that could easily grow to become habit, causing unnecessary tension,

Charlie pointed out his observation and shared that the simple solutions were an open mind and open communication.

While it's not always easy for people to realize their blind spots, let alone agree to change their behavior, in this case, he sensed the team member recognized that his assumptions were often inaccurate. Charlie ran the point home, explaining that assumptions were just a lazy, and often lousy, alternative to simply talking with people - to openly find out what they really thought, felt, or had to offer.

That seemed to resonate when the team member admitted to mindreading in other areas of his life. Recognizing that his habit was unproductive, along with having an easy alternative, he thanked Charlie for the conversation and committed to do better going forward.

Relieved that he had uncovered, and hopefully resolved another issue underlying the feud; And grateful for his team member's willingness to follow his advice, Charlie headed back to his office. Once there, he sent notes to HR about the follow-up conversation he just had. Including his team member's recognition and commitment to replace mindreading with open communication.

By Thursday morning, three of the team's recommendations had already arrived in his inbox, including the collaboration from his two (formerly) feuding team members. Involving the team was definitely the right thing to do.

He skipped his morning rounds, focusing instead on catching up and getting ahead of the communication and admin issues that had to be done for the day and the rest of the week. He wanted to devote his afternoon to reviewing the team's recommendations and preparing for their meeting the next morning.

The rest of the team's recommendations had all arrived by 11 a.m. Everyone had finished on time. "That's a great start!" Charlie thought.

He wanted to make sure he was focused on his task that afternoon. So, at lunch he reviewed his answers to the questions from each of the four steps for changing lanes, especially the last one from Step #4: Change Lanes, where he described the future state.

It read:

- ✓ *"It's three months since the day we started to change lanes and the transformation has been remarkable.*
- ✓ *My team and I are operating with newfound energy, confidence, and the capacity to handle whatever comes our way.*
- ✓ *Productivity has surged as we moved from uncertainty and struggle to clarity and confidence, handling our roles in the acquisition with ease."*

Then he looked at what he had added:

"We are setting a positive example and assisting other teams in the company with our new approach for changing lanes."

He shook his head in amazement, wondering whether Bill's recommendation would have happened anyway, or whether he'd somehow opened the door by adding that final line.

"Be careful what you wish for." Charlie thought to himself, smiling, and shaking his head and he packed up his notes and headed back to the office. He couldn't wait to dig into what the team had sent in.

As he read through everyone's submissions, he was impressed with their vision and the care they had put into describing what they thought could improve, along with their ideas for solutions.

A few had added comments that spotting problems was easier than recommending solutions.

"Welcome to my world," Charlie thought.

But they had persevered and offered solutions, nonetheless. Some were *very* creative.

He noticed that they seemed to be aligning into three categories that he broadly titled: **Communication, Collaboration,** and **Accountability.**

Aside from a few outliers, the team's observations and recommendations remarkably supported the goal and objectives he had set in Step #2 and refined in Step #4. With just a little massaging and some contributions of his own, Charlie felt confident they could craft a collective plan for success.

He had printed them all out, and sorted them now into three piles, with a sticky note title above each one: **Communication, Collaboration,** and **Accountability.**

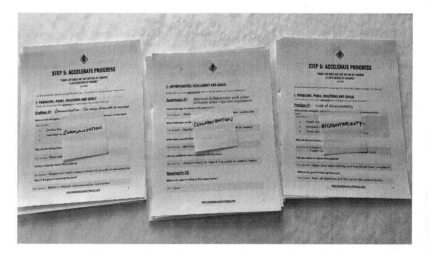

That evening, at dinner with his family, Charlie described the exercise he'd assigned to each member of his team and marveled at how their creative responses lined up with his own priorities to improve engagement, morale, and productivity. His wife commented that the exercise itself might have been a morale booster and offered a few ideas for things he could do at the meeting to bring the *best* out of his team.

She said, "People support what they help to create. They want to see their ideas succeed."

"People support what they help to create."

Which is *exactly* what Charlie was looking for.

He hadn't told his family yet about Bill's request for his team to play a lead role with the acquisition. He wanted to focus first on helping *his* team to change lanes. The outcome of their meeting tomorrow and the following few weeks would determine his answer when Bill returned.

Chapter 14

WISDOM OF THE CROWD

When Friday morning arrived, Charlie followed his plan for the meeting, taking just a few minutes to get things started.

He first removed the mystery, without criticizing, sharing his sense that as a team, they had been operating below their potential in both energy and productivity. Including himself and his own, less-than-ideal, leadership. He then affirmed that he believed in their collective capability and wanted everyone to participate in the solution.

Next, he thanked everyone for their thoughtful contributions, emphasizing the importance of the exercise and the transformation they were striving for.

"I want us realize our true potential," he said to the group, making eye contact as he added, "and I believe you do, too. That's why I've asked for your input, and why we're here today. I want every one of us to be part of the solution. Together we're better than any of us individually." He saw a few heads nodding in agreement.

Next, he explained the process for the meeting. Each member of his team would present their recommendations to the group, describing what they thought could improve and providing their ideas for solutions. They would then take questions and comments until each of their ideas was fully understood.

He added, waving the emails he'd printed, "I've had a chance to look these over, and I have to say that I'm impressed. Every one of these will help us to improve! When all of the presentations are done, we'll discuss them as a group, look for themes, and prioritize the changes that we think will make the most difference."

Charlie started by asking his two (previously) feuding team members to lead off. The others exchanged glances, surprised to see them working together. But they came to the front and took ownership of the situation, explaining that Charlie had asked them to work together, and while it took a bit of reconciliation, they were glad he did. One of them added, jokingly, that, "Believe it or not, we actually agreed with each other's recommendations, and the more we discussed, the more we were able to improve our original ideas for solutions."

They then shared their suggestions. The team asked a few great questions, which they took turns answering. When they were done, Charlie thanked them both, not just for their contributions, but for working together to help the team improve.

That drew a round of applause from the team.

Then he called on the other team members.

As each one spoke, Charlie summarized their solutions on the white board.

At first no one noticed, but they were starting to form three columns.

When they had all finished, Charlie thanked everyone, again, for their thoughtful contributions.

"Before we start to prioritize, let me share what I see," he said, continuing, "When I reviewed your recommendations, I noticed three themes emerging." He spun around and wrote a single word above each column: **Communication, Collaboration**, and **Accountability**.

As Charlie turned back around to face the team, he showed how the recommendations in the first column were all about improving communication: with clients, with other departments, and among the team itself.

The recommendations in the second column were all about collaboration, again with the same three constituencies: clients, other departments, and among the team itself.

And recommendations in the third column called for improvements in accountability.

There were a few outliers, which Charlie had conveniently listed alongside the three columns. He acknowledged that these were worth considering, but he wanted to focus first on the three main themes.

Charlie asked whether anyone on the team had any other observations. They all seemed willing to go along with Charlie's groupings. So, they set about distilling the recommendations for each theme into a single change that they could all agree would be most beneficial for the team's productivity.

After some discussion, they realized that communication and collaboration are really two sides of the same coin. That improving one improved the other. Together, they drafted an agreeable recommendation for both priorities. Then turned their attention to the third priority: accountability.

Charlie said, "Accountability is an interesting subject. It always seems to be in high demand, but short supply..." which drew a few laughs. He continued, "Meaning, we want it from *others*, but fail to see when *we* are coming up short ourselves."

"Improving accountability has two components." Charlie said. "It starts within, by living up to our *own* commitments and having a respectful way to hold others to *their* commitments.

He challenged the team to summarize the three themes, when one said: "*Be accountable for our communication, collaboration, and commitments.*"

Charlie wrote it down, emphasizing each key word.

Another added, "*And hold others to the same standard.*"

Charlie wrote that down, too, underlining "others."

As the team ruminated on the summary, one came up to the board, asked Charlie for the marker, and wrote in huge letters, "**A=C³**," taking the summary to another level.

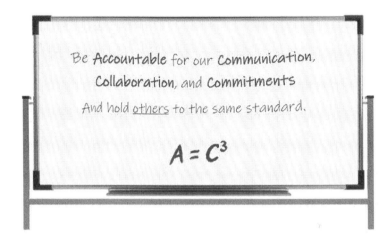

It was brilliant! A mic-drop moment. The room erupted with cheers and high-fives.

The simple formula would make it much easier. Not just to keep their priorities front-of-mind, but to share them with others in the company.

This was an opportunity for every member of the team to take their performance to another level. Charlie *loved* the idea that one of his team members had volunteered about "holding others to the same standard."

He was delighted with how things were turning out. The conversations were inspired and engaging. Everyone seemed to be enthusiastic about delivering on the solutions they had developed and agreed to as a group.

Without knowing it, they were changing lanes and adopting priorities that would fit the role Bill wanted them to play with the acquisition.

Charlie wrapped up the meeting by sharing how impressed he was with the outcome. He said, "This really proves the 'wisdom of the crowd.'" Quoting the legendary business consultant, Ken Blanchard, a motivational speaker, and lead author of the popular *The One Minute Manager* series. Charlie added, "None of us are as smart as all of us."

"None of us are as smart as all of us."
- Ken Blanchard -

He finished by thanking them all again and made a commitment of his own to send a summary of their conclusions before the end of the day.

He asked that everyone respond to that message with an example of one thing *they* could do, immediately, to improve communication, collaboration, and delivering on their commitments.

It would be a great first step for everyone to commit to their new shared priorities while the meeting was fresh in their mind.

Ultimately, though, it would be up to him to make sure the priorities and their commitments remained front-of-mind for everyone going forward.

Over lunch, Charlie made a few notes, summarizing the conclusions and consensus from the meeting, then returned to his office where he wrote and sent his follow-up message to the team:

I want to thank you all again for your inspired contributions at our meeting today. I must say that I am impressed, but not surprised with the outcome we achieved together. Recognizing that we want our team, and everyone on it, to be and do their very best, we are "changing lanes," to be accountable for our communication, collaboration, and commitments. And hold others to the same standard.

Then he typed "$A = C^3$" in big bold type and added: "**SIMPLE is BEST!**"

To get us started in the right direction and stay committed to our commitments, please "reply all" to this memo with one thing you <u>will</u> do, immediately, to improve communication, collaboration, and deliver on your, or our, commitments.

Then he issued a challenge:

Let's see how much progress we can make with our new intentions in the next two weeks. Thank you all again and have a great weekend!

Charlie added a postscript with his own commitments. It read:

"P.S. Here are two things I will do to help us succeed.

1. *Communicate and collaborate with everyone on the team to make sure we individually and collectively deliver on our commitments.*

2. *Assemble the team weekly to drive improved communication and collaboration, and track progress.*

That set a high bar for the team.

Charlie sent the memo, then caught up on email and tasks that had accumulated during their morning meeting. Before leaving for the day, he touched base with everyone, in person, thanking them for their individual contributions and letting them know how valuable they were to him and the team.

He went home for the weekend, feeling great about the meeting and his team's enthusiasm for changing lanes. With a sense of accomplishment, he was able to leave work behind and put his whole focus for the weekend on his family and friends.

RAPID PROGRESS

Gaining Momentum

Chapter 15

FEELING THE DIFFERENCE

On Monday, there was a noticeable difference. By noon, everyone had replied with their commitment to the new lane. The high level of energy around the office was palpable.

"Check," thought Charlie, reflecting on his original goal.

Wanting to maintain the enthusiasm, he made sure to thank everyone for their innovative commitments to changing lanes. He felt it was the beginning of a new level of potential for his team.

By Wednesday, he was noticing more and better communication and visibly more initiative for collaboration with customers, other departments, and especially other members on the team. He sent the team a meeting invitation for Friday morning with an agenda to reconvene and review progress with their new commitment and mantra. He had already seen some behavior and performance changes that he wanted to publicly recognize.

Charlie sent Bill a quick note, letting him know that the meeting had gone well, sharing their new commitment and the formula they had created to remain focused, adding that he was already noticing a difference.

He wrote, "Now, we'll see if we can sustain it." He wished Bill well and promised to stay in touch.

His commitment was to complete this lane change, accelerate progress, and sustain their growing momentum.

Things only got better as the week went on. To be sure, it wasn't all rainbows and unicorns. There had been some challenges and surprises, as usual, and even a few setbacks. But the team had taken them in stride, collaborating and communicating with whomever was necessary to overcome issues and stay on track, often without any input or direction from Charlie.

Friday's meeting took less than 30 minutes. Charlie started by thanking everyone for their new level of energy and diligence, and recognized several team members for new behavior and the extra effort they were making to complete projects and keep their commitments.

Everyone had positive feedback. They discussed a few challenges that members of the team had encountered and solved by engaging with customers and others in the company to improve communication and collaboration: turning problems into opportunities. They all seemed to like being on a team that was determined to improve and determined to succeed.

And it all felt easier.

Charlie closed the meeting with a smile, letting them know how proud he was of their commitment and how grateful he was for the opportunity to work with them on this mission.

It had only been a week since their initial meeting, but Charlie already felt that they had gotten unstuck from the behavior that had been slowing them down and were now making progress in a new lane.

The following week their momentum increased. Not only were several projects finished ahead of time, but Charlie had gotten calls from a few other division heads thanking him for his team's production. One even asked him what he was doing that was making such a difference. "We're changing lanes," was all Charlie said.

By Wednesday, he had seen no signs of progress slowing down, or his team drifting back into their old lane and unproductive ways.

He texted Bill. "I think we're ready.", was all he said. "Let me know when you arrive and let's do dinner. My treat!"

"That's *terrific!*" was Bill's reply, which came almost immediately, followed by his arrival and travel schedule. "Please bring your wife," Bill added. "I haven't seen her in a while, and it would be great to catch up with you both."

Charlie quickly made a reservation for Thursday evening at a place near Bill's hotel and sent him the details. Then he added the time and room info for his team meeting on Friday.

Bill responded, "Let's do something different for the team meeting... Is it possible to get them off-site? Perhaps nearby for a long lunch?"

Charlie thought that was a great idea, so he found a great restaurant nearby and booked a private room.

Next, he emailed his team with the change of plans, letting them know that to celebrate their progress, their Friday meeting would be offsite, and he was treating them to lunch. By the end of the day, everyone had confirmed they were in.

At dinner Thursday evening, Bill started by catching up with Charlie and Jill on both family *and* business matters.

Charlie thanked Bill again for his advice and encouragement about changing lanes, filling him in on the steps he had taken and how well they were working.

Bill liked the approach and wanted to hear more detail about the commitments the team had made to improve. After several examples, he smiled and said, "You know, I wasn't surprised to get your text yesterday. When you *really* do the four steps, the changing lanes approach works *every* time.

"When you *really do* the 4 steps, The Changing Lanes Approach works *every* time."

Then he turned to Jill and let her know how much he enjoyed working with Charlie... That he was impressed, but not surprised, by Charlie's instincts about his team's potential, and his willingness to learn and lead successful change.

In turn, she let Bill know what a difference she had seen in Charlie since their meetings began... That whatever Bill was sharing had replaced frustration and dismay with hope, energy, and determination. She *knew* Charlie was a great leader and was relieved to see him making such progress.

Jill added her appreciation for Bill's coaching, helping Charlie to change lanes at work *and* at home.

Charlie accepted the praise gracefully, but really gave credit to Bill's coaching and the simplicity of his changing lanes approach. Adding that answering the questions and filling out the worksheets for each step had given him the clarity, confidence, and determination to lead the change that he knew they needed, and felt his team was capable of.

The rest of the meal was spent with the three of them talking about the new responsibilities Bill had in store, along with the challenges and priorities Charlie's team would have to deal with.

After learning more about the goal and expectations, Charlie knew it would be a stretch, maybe even a leap. But he was optimistic and confident that his team could, and would, rise to the challenge.

Over dessert, they all discussed what Charlie and Bill would each do at the meeting. Charlie would handle introductions and fill Bill in on their commitments and progress. Then Bill would deliver the news to the team about the new role the company wanted them to play, to help ensure the success of the acquisition.

They bid farewell after the meal, both looking forward to meeting with the team. What Bill didn't share was that he had a few more surprises up his sleeve.

NEW OPPORTUNITY

Another Lane Change

Chapter 16

NEW CHALLENGE

The next day, the energy among the team was infectious. They were winning, and they knew it.

Not only was it Friday, but everyone was excited for their off-site lunch. Charlie had said it was a celebration, and that they were having a guest, so no one expected much work.

By noon they were all seated at the restaurant, with one empty chair remaining. Charlie let the team know that in addition to celebrating their success, one of his commitments was to bring in other leaders to share strategy and give everyone an opportunity to understand their priorities in the company.

At that moment, almost as if choreographed, Bill made his entrance, wearing a huge smile. But he was not alone. Right beside him was Liz, the company president.

Charlie was stunned, as was the team. The room grew silent for a moment before Bill broke the ice. He said to Charlie and the team, "Thank you for having me! I hope you don't mind, but when I arrived this morning, I found that our president didn't have any lunch plans, so I invited her to join us. And I think she has something to share."

Charlie was surprised, but happily so. He quickly arranged for another chair, and they all got settled in ordering a few appetizers to get started.

Then Charlie rose to make introductions.

Addressing his team, he said, "Liz, of course, is our president. If you haven't had a chance to talk with her, I can tell you that she would like to talk with you. She is a 'people-first' leader, which starts with us, and extends to the people in the companies we serve. Her vision and direction are directly responsible for the growth and success we've enjoyed in the last 10 years."

Liz nodded with a smile and gracefully replied, deflecting the compliment. "Thank you, Charlie, but our success is *really* because of inspired teams like you-all," she said gesturing around the table, continuing, "who embrace our vision and overcome challenges *every* day to help others in the market."

The team all sat a little taller. If they didn't appreciate her before, they certainly did now, thought Charlie.

He thanked her for joining them, then said, "Next, if you don't know him, you may know *of* him. Bill used to run our division and is the very first person I met when I started here years ago. He was soon promoted to vice president of business development, and now serves as senior vice president leading all business development efforts. He reports directly to Liz."

"That initial meeting was a turning point in my career as Bill quickly became both a friend and mentor." He continued, looking at Bill. "A benefit that I'm sure is shared by many others in the company."

Bill blushed slightly but smiled and nodded with pride and appreciation. Charlie continued, "We had fallen out of touch since Bill relocated, but reunited a few weeks ago, over lunch, when he was visiting for a recent board meeting. In fact, *he* is the main reason we are all here today."

Bill was curious how Charlie would lay this out for his team.

He said, "The shift in my attitude and energy… the one you have all picked-up and run with, accelerating our progress and productivity… is *all* because of a simple lesson Bill shared with me about changing lanes."

"The success of his advice, and how well you have all responded, is why we're celebrating."

"Well, that's not the *only* reason." Bill said, standing as he did. "I'm sure, by now, you're all aware of our recent acquisition." The team looked around nodding. They had read the internal memos and seen occasional reports in the local news.

"The talent and customer base from the acquisition both complement our own, and significantly extend the value we can provide to both current and new customers. This acquisition brings the potential to *accelerate* our progress and propel us to the front of the markets we collectively serve."

"As you know," Bill continued, "merging cultures successfully is both delicate and essential for an acquisition to succeed. That is why we would like *you*," he said, pausing for effect, looking first at Charlie, then at everyone around the table, "and your team, to lead the merging of the two cultures."

Knowing this was coming, Charlie smiled, and took in the stunned faces around the room.

Now Liz stood and took the floor. Smiling, she looked first at Charlie and said, "We've had our eye on all of you, for some time," Now looking around the room. "As we were contemplating the acquisition, we knew it would take a team of front-line influencers to really bring the best of both cultures together.

"Every team goes through peaks and valleys, through lulls and surges. As Bill kept me informed about how you've embraced and applied the changing lanes approach to improve your own productivity, I was willing to bet we had our winner. When he shared your goals and rapid progress with the board, the vote was unanimous.

"You see, both companies are changing lanes right now, merging, really, into a new lane that will allow us to go farther and faster than either company could go before.

"Who better to bring that about than a team that's doing it themselves?"

The team was clearly excited by the news, but somewhat mystified about this "changing lanes approach." All they knew was that they had responded to Charlie's requests and heard him mention changing lanes a few times.

Liz continued. "We've never had a team or department dedicated to organizational development. But with the success of this acquisition at stake, the board thinks we should give it a try. And we agree!"

"In fact," Liz added, "Bill was actually the champion of the idea. Succeeding with the acquisition is our top priority, and this team is the one we want to lead the way. If you accept, of course.

It sounded like a great challenge and assignment. Charlie looked at his team and asked, "Well, what do you say? Is everyone on board?"

Heads were nodding, and many team members were giving the thumbs-up. He looked at Liz and Bill and said, "There's your answer... We're in!"

Liz addressed the room: "We'll get together early next week to share our goals and priorities. We want to get your input on that as well. All of you," she added. "Along with what you'll need in the way for resources and support to succeed. There will also be new terms and incentives for each of you, which I'm confident you will like. Bill and I have both gone out of our way to make sure of that."

As she and Bill were speaking, refreshments had arrived and the food was on its way. With Liz's comment about the new goals and terms, the two formerly feuding team members, who were seated together, both raised their glasses, and one offered a toast: "To our new mission." Bill joined in, "To our new team!"

While he knew his leadership was heading for a growth spurt, Charlie didn't want to miss the moment, and he added, "To our new lane, and achieving our goals!"

The glasses all met, and the food arrived. As the meal went on, conversation went back and forth with questions and answers that not only revealed the steps and simplicity of the changing lanes approach, but also began to shape their ideas and plans to sustain progress and gain momentum as the two companies became one.

Before the meeting was done, Liz had spoken personally with each member of the team, with Bill often joining her. She seemed to know a bit about each person and was genuinely interested in their thoughts about the value of the acquisition and the importance of their new roles. It was another example of her excellent leadership.

Charlie remembered Bill's advice from Step #4, that it was imperative for a leader to be visible when leading change. He saw that both Liz and Bill were involving the team in shaping the how and when of the lane change and wondered whether Bill had learned changing lanes from Liz, or Liz had learned it from Bill. He would find out later, but it was on full display. And it was working.

It is **imperative** to be visible when leading change.

Then it struck Charlie that the acquisition, this lunch, and the promotion of his team were all part of a *major* lane change for the company. One that was happening carefully, but thoughtfully.

"Change really *doesn't* have to be hard," thought Charlie. "Even at this scale... just follow the same four steps we all do when driving. Or *should* do," he corrected himself, to change lanes and go from where we are to where we want to be.

After lunch, they all strolled back to the office. Bill and Liz bid farewell, and Charlie asked the team for a quick huddle in the conference room to share his thoughts and answer a few questions about the next steps.

When they assembled, he said, "I want you all to know how proud I am of this team, and every one of you for how well you've responded to changing lanes. This is the reward we've received for all committing to be part of the solution." That drew a round of cheers and applause.

"Things are going to move quickly," said Charlie. "Monday and Tuesday will be business as usual, so make progress on your current projects. Some, you may hand off. Some you may finish. Our transition won't be like a light switch, but it won't be a slow dimmer either.

"The board wants us to be fully functional in our new roles within two weeks. I will be coming around Monday and Tuesday with Bill and someone from HR to visit with each of you about your new responsibilities, expectations, performance requirements, incentive compensation, and benefits."

"Assuming that goes well, you'll be part of a team meeting on Wednesday afternoon to brainstorm our approach and plan our launch the following week."

He finished by saying, "You've just had a lot dropped on you. To your credit, you've been wonderfully positive about it all. Why don't you wrap-up for the day and go enjoy your weekend. If you have any questions or concerns, just reach out. I don't mind a call over the weekend. I want you all to enjoy what's about to become our new lane and be prepared to bring your best ideas and energy to our transition next week."

"I'm going to draft some steps for our new lane change and will be looking for input from each of you next week before our meeting on Wednesday." He could see a few quizzical looks, like they didn't understand. He assured them, "Don't worry. You'll be surprised how simple it will be."

"Now go," he concluded.

With that, they all left, smiling, and obviously energized.

Charlie went back to his office, opened a *new* set of worksheets for their next goal, which he listed as: "Lead Successful Acquisition."

He spent just 10 minutes capturing his initial thoughts on the questions for each step. In less than an hour, he had gained clarity on the challenge and was confident that using the changing lanes approach, his team would succeed with the transformation. He was looking forward to sharing the process and getting their input.

With that bit of progress, he cleared his desk and couldn't wait to get home. It *would* be a great weekend!

He drove home, almost unconsciously, lost in thought as he re-played conversations and moments from the lunch and had his own imagination racing about the weeks ahead. He was changing lanes instinctively, always into one that was moving better than the one he'd been in. When he realized what had been going on, he wondered whether it might be an omen for the future. He just smiled at the happy thought and finished his drive with his mind on the road.

Charlie couldn't wait for dinner to share the good news with his family. They knew from conversations earlier in the week that today had been the day the team would get the news. Over dinner, Charlie shared that the company president herself had shown up and surprised them with a big announcement, making their team the new Department of Organizational Development.

His wife smiled and said with a big smile, "Congratulations!"

The kids wanted to know what organizational development was, so Charlie filled them in on how they would be working with teams from both companies to merge capabilities and foster collaboration that would help everyone excel and help the whole company to grow and succeed.

The following week, as Charlie made his rounds with the team, he shared a quick explanation of the changing lanes approach and asked their input on some of the questions he had answered with his draft. Afterward, he sent them clean worksheets for changing lanes that they could use to collect *their* thoughts prior to the Wednesday meeting.

His only instruction was: "Imagine you're in charge. How would you answer each question if you wanted our team to succeed with this challenge, on time, or ahead of time."

With that, he added, "Just reach out, or come and see me, if you have any questions or want to brainstorm. You can also do that with each other."

While there was some uncertainty, "Like making your first lane change on a highway as a new driver," Charlie thought, they all were glad to have some steps to follow rather than trying to figure it out on their own.

He decided it would be a good idea to assemble the team on Tuesday afternoon, for a quick huddle. It would give him a chance to see how they were responding to the questions before the Wednesday meeting with Liz and Bill. And also, to validate their individual ideas and approach the meeting with some consensus and confidence, rather than trepidation or uncertainty.

For two reasons, Charlie scheduled the Tuesday huddle during the last hour of the day.

One was to give everyone as much time as possible to consider the questions from each of the four Steps.

The other reason was that he didn't want the meeting to drift or to drag on. Scheduling it at the end of the day guaranteed they would finish on time. He really just wanted the team to gain perspective from their colleagues and see what insight and solutions they could bring to the meeting on Wednesday.

Liz had circulated a memo first thing Monday morning, announcing their team's new focus on organization development. Along with their mission and priorities - and letting everyone in both companies know that Charlie's team would be in touch with their departments to solicit input and assistance.

After meeting with each of his team members to help them understand the changing lanes approach, Charlie reached out to several peers running other departments and divisions to get their ideas and perspectives on how to help make the acquisition a success and merge the best of the two business cultures. They all congratulated him on the new assignment, and most were more than willing to help.

Some had ideas on the spot. Others scheduled a call back later in the day or on Tuesday. Some were swamped and said, "maybe by the end of the week." "That was a clue," thought Charlie. If somehow, the acquisition could lighten the load of those already swamped, it would be a win-win. He made a note to think it over and even bring it up in the meeting on Wednesday.

Tuesday's huddle went extremely well. He fielded some insightful questions and ideas from each team member prior to the meeting and could see there was both diversity *and* consensus in their thinking. Both were essential for their success.

In less than an hour, they had listed their questions, concerns, and initial ideas and inspirations for the meeting Wednesday.

Charlie didn't know if he was more impressed with the collective wisdom of his team or the foresight Liz and Bill had for assigning a team, in this case *his* team, to the task of accelerating the success of the acquisition.

Chapter 17

NEW PLAN

Liz took charge of Wednesday's meeting. Bill was also there with the two new board members from the acquired company. After the introductions, Liz confirmed that everyone was on board for their new roles and expressed her appreciation that they had accepted the challenge.

She laid out her vision for how the two companies could come together and become a market leader. Where there would be overlap and where there might be gaps. She then led a Q & A session before taking any suggestions or recommendations.

The goal of the meeting was to draft a fully informed plan that the team could begin to act upon immediately.

When Liz opened the discussion up, Charlie's team was ready. Their questions quickly revealed priorities, uncertainties, and challenges that would require the most immediate attention.

After 40 minutes, with all questions asked and answered, they took a quick break and returned to take recommendations and draft a six-month action plan, including specific goals and objectives.

The time his team had spent preparing and considering questions from the four steps of changing lanes had really paid off. Each of his team members made meaningful observations and suggestions that Bill wrote on the whiteboard along with those from leaders of the acquired company, some of his own, and a few from Liz herself. It had been a true brainstorming session.

When the room fell silent, Charlie spotted a way to connect the dots. He stood to take the marker and began circling and linking items that Bill had written, explaining as he went and distilling them into a new list with three priorities and several subtasks for each one. It would simplify and bring order to what had previously grown into a daunting list of competing priorities.

With some additional discussion and eventual agreement from the room, they identified milestones and target dates for each of the tasks and priorities.

Charlie offered that members of his team would be assigned in pairs to each of the tasks, along with mentors from the leadership teams of both companies whom they would count on for support and assistance.

That finished, Charlie went back to his seat, and Liz returned to the front. She asked Charlie to write up the draft plan and circulate it for any additional comments, then shared a three-point game plan for how they would proceed:

1. She wanted the plan firmed up by Friday morning, so everyone could get underway the following week.

2. They would have virtual status meetings weekly, to report and discuss progress or challenges with their tasks and priorities. And,

3. There would be live monthly meetings, with team members inviting anyone else from either company who had something useful to offer or had helped with progress to achieve any of the milestones.

Charlie thought that was a brilliant way to bring the two cultures together on common goals and keep everyone's focus on the new priorities.

Liz asked if there were any final questions or concerns. After a brief silence, one of his team members raised a hand. She said, "This looks like a great plan, but many of the people we'll be working with we don't even know. What happens if we run into reluctance or resistance?"

"Great question!" said Liz. "Two things:

"One: I have already circulated a company-wide memo letting everyone know that your team has been appointed to bring the best of the cultures together and accelerate the success of the acquisition. I will continue to reinforce that with bi-weekly updates.

"Two: You have the four of us who you can turn to for assistance and support," gesturing to her and Bill and the two leaders of the acquired company."

"And three!" said Bill. "I have a resource I can share with each of you. It's a helpful guide with *5 Solutions to Reduce or Eliminate Resistance to Change*. Read it and use it. I'm sure you will find it helpful."

Then he added, "With the changing lanes approach, you should see as much buy-in and support as we've enjoyed from each of you."

171

With that final question answered, Liz thanked everyone for their thoughtful contributions and adjourned the meeting.

Charlie went back to his office to type and distribute the draft action plan. He shared the four worksheets for changing lanes with members of his team again, and asked each of them to prepare answers for their assigned tasks once the action plan was finalized on Friday. Adding that he would review each step with them in their assigned pairs on Monday morning.

Just after he pressed send, a group message came through from Bill with his own personal thanks for everyone's contributions along with a link to the guide he had promised.

5-Solutions-for-Overcoming-Resistance-to-Change

"It looks like we're underway!" said Charlie, out loud to himself.

THE
TRANSFORMATION

Achieving Goals

Chapter 18

AHEAD OF EXEPTACTIONS

The last six months had been a blur. Liz's plans for weekly progress meetings and monthly milestone get-togethers had worked brilliantly.

At first their focus had been on granular issues that arose when their plan met the reality of inertia from both companies and people's reluctant to change.

But true to her word, assistance from Liz and the other company leaders, along with his team's use of the changing lanes approach, and the success they realized with Bill's helpful guide, had quickly turned resistance into support.

His team made a practice of inviting a guest from the company leadership team, other departments, suppliers, and even customers to join them every other week, to offer the team an on-going view of reality from *their* perspective. It turned out to be a real game-changer, helping them to avoid 'groupthink' and tunnel vision.

Inviting guests to the monthly meetings revealed enthusiastic new leadership candidates just in time to help with the company's growth. As teams and projects had been realigned and reassigned, they achieved one milestone after another, missing only one and getting the others accomplished on time or ahead of time.

Liz and Bill had decided that this month's milestone meeting, on the six-month anniversary of the acquisition, would be off-site.

Charlie found himself back at the same restaurant where his team had been tasked with their new focus on organizational development. They had truly grown into the new role, accelerating the development of people and processes well beyond their initial charge of merging the best of the two cultures.

While they had encountered many challenges, the team's can-do mindset had always prevailed. Like driving, they changed lanes often to maintain progress whenever they encountered a slow-down or obstacle, coming up with at least three solutions for every issue.

After everyone was seated and refreshments had arrived, Liz stood to start the conversation. She reminded everyone that it had been just six months since the acquisition, then cited the many milestones achieved and progress generated thanks to everyone's contributions.

The transformation was working. The company had begun to grow and was already moving into a market leadership role.

She said, "Everyone here has made a significant contribution, but one person's leadership provided the spark that has ignited and sustained our progress and success." Charlie already knew she was talking about Bill.

Then she turned to Charlie and said, "When we saw the transformation you made with your team, we believed we had the right group and leader to combine the two cultures," she said looking around the table. "And we were right!" she said, looking back at

Charlie. "With your inspiration and your team's dedication, we are making great progress and are ahead of *every* expectation we had for the acquisition."

She added, "We want to continue on that same trajectory."

Then Bill stood to join the conversation, looked directly at Charlie, and said, "Which is why we want to make this team's assignment permanent and promote *you* to VP of Organizational Development."

Charlie was stunned. He had *not* seen this coming.

He looked back to Bill who said, "Don't look at me. It was her idea!" he said gesturing to Liz, who had a huge smile on her face.

It took Charlie a minute to form a question, "So, this is *really* a permanent promotion for the *whole* team?"

"Yes!" Liz and Bill said in unison.

Then Liz added, just in case Charlie had missed it, "And *you* too!"

The team erupted in cheers and applause. They had grown to enjoy their role of accelerating the company's development and were excited about the opportunity to stick with it and see just how far they could go.

Then one of his team members raised a glass, looked at Charlie, and said "Congratulations on the VP role! Well deserved!"

The rest of the room joined the toast.

When Charlie finally got a chance to speak, he stood and said, after some hesitation, "I am honored. But I need to give credit where credit is due."

He turned and said "Bill, it was your insight and timely coaching about changing lanes that really provided the spark for our transformation." Bill simply nodded back in appreciation.

Then Charlie added, looking back to the room, "And especially to my team! Your willingness and enthusiasm to lead change has been an inspiration. I believe in each of you, and I believe in what we can accomplish together. But there is no way I will take this role unless you are all with me. Those are *my* terms," he said, completing his challenge.

One-by-one, they all raised their glasses and said, "I'm in!".

One team member even kidded that they didn't want to see Charlie fail in his new role, so they would agree to *sacrifice* and stay with him. That drew laughs all around as Charlie turned back to Liz and Bill and said, "Well, that seals it. If they won't let me fail, then I accept!" He added, with a huge smile of his own. "Thank you for the opportunity."

They shook hands and shared a few hugs. Then the rest of the lunch continued as more of a celebration than a meeting.

The announcement itself was a milestone marking their rapid progress and making organizational development a permanent assignment.

Charlie took the opportunity to move about the room to thank each member of the team and each of the guests for their hard work and contributions. He spent extra time with Liz and Bill, expressing his appreciation more deeply for their guidance and support, and committing to future success.

They spoke for a while longer before Bill said, "Charlie, don't forget about the next step." Charlie paused for a second, remembering what he had come to call the "5th step" of the changing lanes approach, a tradition that would continue to move the company forward and help to gain even more momentum.

He smiled at Bill and said, "I think you're right… It's time!"

Charlie turned to get everyone's attention and said, "Now that the two companies are united and making progress, it's time to focus forward.

"For my first official act as VP of organizational development, I'd like to start a new tradition." This drew a few eye rolls and comical groans from the crowd.

Charlie smiled and continued. "It's one I think you'll enjoy, and one that is *sure* to accelerate our progress and help us become a market leader." Now they were all curious.

"Prior to next month's milestone meeting I would like everyone here to submit a problem we still have that you believe we should overcome, or an opportunity you see that we can seize, along with at least two ideas for solutions on how to do so.

"We'll review everyone's recommendations at next month's meeting and decide which ones to act on and when.

"I will send more info in the week ahead, but this exercise is one we will continue at least twice each year. Rather than waiting to *cope* with change, this tradition will have us out *looking* for it to gain momentum and become a true market leader."

Around the room, he saw approving nods, a few quizzical looks, and many confident smiles. He knew the team would enjoy the challenge and be up to the task.

With that said, Charlie had set in motion a process to accelerate progress with the changing lanes approach. This process would inspire and challenge his team, and the entire company for that matter, to *reliably* generate a successful future.

As the lunch meeting wound down, Liz encouraged everyone to address any critical items or communication, then knock-off early for the day. You've all earned a break." she said. "Take the rest of your day and enjoy it." That drew another cheer from the group.

As they made their way back to the office. Charlie knew that some of his team would stay and work. They truly loved what they were doing. While that was also true for Charlie, he couldn't wait to get home and share the great news with his family.

He cleared his desk, decided that his email with instructions for the Bonus Step could wait until Monday, then set his out-of-office reminder for email and headed for the door.

On the way home, still reeling with excitement about his promotion and the future of his team, he was keenly aware of how effortless it had become for him to spot opportunities to change lanes. To maintain his progress and even accelerate when others were dealing with slowdowns.

He shook his head at the transformation he, his team, and the whole company had enjoyed over the past 6-8 months... From frustration and disappointment to enthusiasm and achievement.

The simple solution had been there, right in front of him, the whole time:

Changing Lanes for Business.

When he got home the house was empty. The kids weren't home from school yet, and he guessed his wife was still with her client. One-by-one, they all arrived home, excited for the weekend. Jill came in carrying flowers. When he asked what she'd gotten flowers for, she replied "Oh nothing. I got them myself. I just wanted to brighten the place-up a bit."

He called them all together in the kitchen for the big announcement that his team had earned a permanent assignment with *him* as the new vice president!

The kids were excited, jumping, screaming and high fiving their dad. His wife smiled, reached over, handed him the flowers, and said with a big smile, "Congratulations!"

He took the flowers, suspiciously, and said, "Wait, did you *know* about this?"

Still smiling, she said, "Yes. But *they* didn't," nodding at the kids who were still jumping around.

She added, "Bill called this morning to let me know about the promotions he and Liz had planned for you and your team. I think it's terrific… You've *earned* it!"

"Thank you!" he replied.

Jill said, "I let Bill know how much you value his coaching and how you'd been sharing what you'd learned at dinners with the family. I mentioned how simple the changing lanes approach seemed and asked where I could learn about it to share with my clients.

"He said that he just finished writing a book, complete with the worksheets he's had you doing, and online resources to help business leaders with a simple and reliable way to succeed with change. He's had a few trial copies printed, but asked if *I* would help to publish it!

"That's *great!*" exclaimed Charlie.

Jill replied, "That's not all." Then paused for effect, adding: "*We* are the main characters in his book!"

"Wait," said Charlie. "He wrote about *us?!*"

She continued, "Of course, he changed our names, but he said that fundamentally, the story was about a talented but struggling business leader, facing adversity, and often a string of frustrating issues and challenges.

"He explained that most often progress, and even *huge* success, in business is found by simply '*changing lanes*' in one direction or another.

"He said that his first copy would be for you, since your meetings and application of the steps had happened just as he was finishing the book."

"I guess I'm honored." said Charlie, recalling that Bill had mentioned he was "working on something."

After a long pause he cracked, "I wonder who they'll get to play me in the movie?"

Jill thought for a moment and said, "Probably Homer Simpson." putting him in his place. Then she added, for emphasis, "The resemblance is *just* too hard to ignore!"

The kids were howling and agreed with mom.

Then grinning, she said, "Hey Homer, Let's go out to dinner. It's time to celebrate and I don't feel like cooking!"

He gave her another big hug and a kiss, then gathered up the kids to start the weekend with a nice family meal.

Even through a fun and relaxing weekend with his family, Charlie couldn't help but think about the new challenges and opportunities ahead for him and his team. He journaled about several ideas and inspirations and also about how he could get everyone in the company onboard with changing lanes.

Chapter 19

TO YOUR AMAZING FUTURE!

By Monday morning, he was eager to get to work where he could make progress in his new lane. His first order of business was to send a heartfelt thank you note to every member of his team, especially to Liz and Bill. For occasions like this, handwritten notes were 100 times better than email.

He had no sooner finished when he looked up and noticed Bill at his office door, along with his carry-on luggage. Charlie invited him in and said, "Perfect timing. You saved me a stamp." handing him the note. "What's with the luggage?"

Bill explained that with his work in town finished, he was headed back home to explore some new opportunities the company was considering, but that he didn't want to leave without stopping to say goodbye in person.

"And to give you this," Bill said as he reached into his bag and handed Charlie his new book, titled *Changing Lanes for Business*.

Charlie accepted it with a smile and said, "I heard there was a book deal in the works!"

"Yes," Bill replied, "Jill has agreed to publish it! This is the very first copy, and I want you to have it."

Charlie was truly touched. He laid the book on his desk alongside the stack of original wrinkled worksheets he'd completed for each of the four steps. There would be a new one added today for the Bonus Step.

Charlie said, "The Changing Lanes Approach is truly a path to progress!"

Pointing at the papers, he added, "I still refer to these all the time. The clarity and confidence these simple steps develop is priceless! I've decided to have these original worksheets framed and hung right there on my wall for everyone to see. The genesis of our transformation."

Then he looked back at Bill and said, "None of this would have happened without your wisdom and impeccable timing."

Bill dismissed the compliment and said, "You would have found a way to succeed Charlie. I just helped you with a simple approach that works."

They talked a while longer about how Bill had discovered and refined his approach. How well Charlie had applied it with his team. And through them, with other leaders and departments across the company.

Bill wrapped up the conversation brilliantly.

"Charlie, I know you've heard me say that the one constant in business is change. I also know that leading successful change is *the* most valuable skill in the market today!

Leading successful change is *the* most valuable skill in the market today!

"There is no reason for you, or *any* business leader, to *ever* be trapped or stuck for very long with problems or lack of progress. If you want to succeed in the coming month, the coming year, or for the rest of your career, *you can do that*. You can improve *any* situation you choose.

"Just follow the four simple steps for changing lanes for a reliable path to progress... to gain clarity, confidence, and support for the changes you want to make. That will put you, your team, and your business in position to make progress and achieve your goals."

Charlie looked him in the eye and said, "*You can count on it!*"

With that, Bill stood to leave.

Charlie walked him to the door, shook his hand and thanked him one last time for his guidance, and especially the thoughtful book. They promised to stay in touch as they both *changed lanes* to achieve success.

After seeing Bill off, Charlie returned to the book and opened the cover, where he found an inscription:

Charlie,

Your interest, initiative, and determination to suc-
ceed has been the inspiration for this book. You have
brought Changing Lanes for Business to life, and for
that I am truly grateful... To your amazing future!
Bill

Below there was a postscript, which read,
See you in the fast lane!

Smiling, he said out loud, "We're already in the fast lane, thanks to you!"

For more on Changing Lanes for Business, visit:
www.ChangingLanesApproach.com

For 5 Solutions to Reduce or Eliminate Resistance to Change,
visit: www.bit.ly/Resistance-to-Change-Guide

All progress

Change Lanes to make rapid progress and achieve your goals in life and business.

Step #1: DECIDE to Change

Not deciding to change is actually one of the biggest reasons why critical changes fail to happen in business. Uncertain about what to do, lacking resources, clarity, or support, many leaders simply remain stuck.

Answer the questions in Step #1 to gain immediate clarity about what you want, why, and how you can get there. Then DECIDE to Change.

Step #2: LOOK for Options and Risks

Look for opportunities to Change Lanes that will improve progress and accelerate your success.

Involve others to build support and confidence. Understand what's in place to support your change as well as any obstacles or people you'll have to overcome to succeed.

Now turn your decision into a commitment. Answer the questions from Step #2 to understand the options and risks and make sure the path you're planning is clear and safe.

Learn more at: **ChangingLanesApproach.com**
Use Promo Code: **CHARLIE** to Save 20%

requires change.

Step #3: SIGNAL the Change

"Poor communication is the root of every problem."

Letting everyone involved know that the change is coming, why it is important or beneficial, and what they can or must do to make it succeed, is essential.

Create your Signal the Change Checklist so you will know who, how and when to best signal - to avoid problems, gain support and be a "success-maker".

Step #4: CHANGE LANES

Now, it's time to act... To implement your plans for change.

Complete your Changing Lanes Roadmap, listing the steps to start and finish your change.

Then turn the wheel. Step on the gas and move into the new lane. Make rapid progress with your team or project and accelerate toward the goal.

Express appreciation and give credit to others for their commitment and contributions. Celebrate wins as you achieve success.

Leading productive change is the most valuable skill and talent in the market today.

Start Changing Lanes now to get from where you are to where you want to be.

Praise for The Changing Lanes Coaching Program:

"Hands-down the easiest, step-by-step coaching program to lead successful change and position your business or project for success!"

"Changing Lanes is a quick, efficient way to learn a basic approach to change that anyone can execute!"

"Changing Lanes produces results, PERIOD! It is by far the most valuable program/workshop I have experienced, and I have participated in many throughout my career."

"I am amazed at the successful outcomes in our organization."

"Changing Lanes helped us to take our culture to the next level!"

Changing Lanes For Business Coaching Program

Learn the 4 Simple Steps to Accelerate Progress and Achieve Your Goals!

✔ **Leadership Growth**
Gain clarity, confidence & courage to do what's necessary

✔ **Team Development**
Improve team, culture and front-line engagement

✔ **Financial Gains**
Generate rapid 5, 6, and even 7-figure gains

✔ **Increase Market Share**
Overcome problems and innovate to become a market leader.

Lead Successful Change with Confidence!

Learn more at: **ChangingLanesApproach.com**
Use Promo Code: **CHARLIE** to Save 20%

INDEX

Whose help will you need 66
Whose permission will you need 66
why he hadn't taken action sooner 107
why start if you don't 'plan' to finish 83
willingness to learn and lead successful
        change 152
Will it save time or take your time 48
working for his team, rather than the
        other way around 66

Y

You never learn anything like when you
        teach it 128
You're at A. Where's B 29
You're worth it 45
you've got to care 62

ACKNOWLEDGMENTS

This book is a culmination of the experience, support, wisdom, and inspiration provided by countless incredible individuals.

My family, Liz, TJ and Jake, my partners in life, have been an ever-present force of love, sacrifice, and encouragement. Their belief in me, and my dedication to them, has kept me moving forward through life's many challenges, opportunities and lane changes.

My many mentors, whose timely guidance and wisdom I have been fortunate to apply and share over the years. I stand on the shoulders of giants, and you will find many of their priceless lessons shining through these pages.

My colleagues and teammates, for thinking differently, and encouraging me to do the same. For always trying new things, and constantly raising the bar to exceed expectations.

The precious clients and customers who, over the years, have placed their trust in our potential and ability to help them achieve new levels of success.

And finally, Kelli, Greg, and the talented team with **Scriptor Publishing** who have helped to transform an innovative approach into an inspiring story - with the potential to help leaders make progress for years to come.

To each and every one of you, from the depths of my heart, thank you.

ABOUT THE AUTHOR

Tim Rhode is a highly successful business consultant, author, motivational speaker, and leadership coach with more than 35 years of entrepreneurial experience. He has personally launched and led multiple 7 and 8-figure high-service-level businesses, helping tens of thousands of customers, and hundreds of team members to transform their lives, both personally and professionally.

Since 2015, he's coached and consulted leaders and teams in dozens of industries to overcome challenges and get from where they are now—to where they want to be.

Tim does this by offering inspiration, new perspectives, and new ideas to overcome limiting beliefs and roadblocks. To accelerate growth, success, and abundance.

His extensive experience and ability to relate to other business leaders allow him to effectively coach others through helpful changes that dramatically improve their revenue, profit, and culture.

Made in the USA
Columbia, SC
19 December 2024

49898063R00117